A Ghost Called Dog

Gavin Neale

2QT Limited (Publishing)

First Edition published 2016
2QT Limited (Publishing)
Settle, North Yorkshire BD24 9RH
www.2qt.co.uk

Copyright © Gavin Neale 2016
The right of Gavin Neale to be identified as the author of this work has been asserted by him in accordance with the Copyright, Designs and Patents Act 1988

All rights reserved. This book is sold subject to the condition that no part of this book is to be reproduced, in any shape or form. Or by way of trade, stored in a retrieval system or transmitted in any form or by any means, electronic, mechanical, photocopying, recording, be lent, re-sold, hired out or otherwise circulated in any form of binding or cover other than that in which it is published and without a similar condition, including this condition being imposed on the subsequent purchaser, without prior permission of the copyright holder.

Illustrations by ©Rose Hutchings

Author/Publisher disclaimer:
This book is a work of fiction. Names, characters, places and incidents are the product of the author's imagination. Any resemblance to actual persons living or dead, events or locales is entirely coincidental.

Printed in Great Britain by Lightning Source UK Ltd

A CIP catalogue record for this book is available
from the British Library
ISBN 978-1-910077-78-8

*For my grandmothers Daphne and Nora,
who taught me more important things than magic*

Prologue

Christopher and Abigail were really not sure about their new house. It smelt funny. It was too clean. And even though their parents had worked ever so hard over many weeks to arrange the move, it seemed strange to go to so much trouble given how nice their old home had been.

Christopher missed the park round the corner with the goal posts where his dad had taught him to play football. Abigail missed the tree at the end of the garden that she loved to climb. In the old house there were places for all of their toys, even the ones buried in the garden. They knew how to make a tent in the bedroom they used to share, and how to squeeze into the cupboard in the dining room when playing hide and seek. The new house was big and strange, with shiny clean surfaces that Mum and Dad were so cross about when you drew on them.

What they didn't realise was that what turns a house into a home is all the good things, bad things, boring things – and sometimes horrifying things – that happen in them when you have lived there for a while.

If Christopher and Abigail had known what was about to happen to them, maybe they would have been a little happier with the nice clean house they had just moved into.

A Ghost called Dog

CHAPTER 1

A Strange Conversation

'Mum, he punched me.'

A tired-looking woman in smart clothes stuck her head round the door and frowned at her two children. She had short brown hair, blue eyes, and was only a little taller than her eleven-year-old son.

'She was kicking me,' Christopher whined.

'Only the once,' said Abigail sullenly.

'Abby, there is really no excuse for attacking your brother, even only once. And Chris, you should know better. Now what's going on?'

'I haven't got enough room,' Abby said, waving her legs around and taking the opportunity to kick her brother again.

'Why don't you move to the end of the sofa, Chris, and then there's room for both of you? And Abby, if you kick your brother once more I'm going to give you a time out before you've even had breakfast. Speaking of which, what are you two doing watching TV at this time of the morning?'

'Dad was up,' said Chris, taking on the role of spokesperson. 'He said we could.'

'Hmm,' was all Mum said in reply before walking

away down the hall while her children giggled in the front room.

* * *

'Morning, love,' Mum said to Dad, who was huddled over a laptop on the kitchen table, frantically tapping the keyboard in between sips of coffee.

'Mehua,' he grunted in reply

'I thought you said you were ready for this deadline.' Mum sounded exasperated. 'Tony?'

'Sorry, dear,' said Dad, head jerking round in surprise like a startled deer.

'Did you even go to bed last night?'

'I'm late for my deadline. All this moving and looking after the kids…' he started defensively.

'They've only just come back from their grandparents.' Mum was clearly annoyed. 'And if you hadn't spent so much time working on their bit of the garden, you might have made your deadline for once.'

'Nobody expects me to hit a deadline,' Dad said, to much giggling from the doorway, 'Art does not have a timetable.'

'Come in,' said Mum to the kids, flashing a 'we are not finished yet' look at her husband before turning to face her children.

'Are you going to tell Daddy off?' Abby asked with relish.

Abigail was seven years old, average height for her age, with long brown hair and blue eyes with brown rings around the pupils. She had freckles across her nose and a mischievous, gap-toothed grin. She never walked anywhere

Chapter 1

if she could cartwheel or run and she was utterly fearless in the face of heights, trees and ways to get her brother into trouble. She also loved him very much.

Although Christopher was four years older, he always followed behind her as if he knew who was in charge. He was short for his age and slightly solemn. He had the same brown hair as his sister, but cut short, and his eyes were brown like his father's.

'No, Abby,' said Mum. 'He's been up all night working and you two took advantage of his tiredness, didn't you?'

'Mum...' they chorused.

'Did Daddy actually say you could watch TV or was he working and not paying attention?'

'He was working,' said Chris, realising the game was up and it was time to admit defeat.

'Right, no more TV for today – and that includes the games console.' Mum knew her son liked to play football games as much as kick a ball.

'Mum,' Abby and Chris whined in unison.

'No, you know the rules. In any case, it's going to be a lovely day and there might be a surprise for you in the garden.'

Abby and Chris had been away visiting their grandparents for two weeks while their parents moved into the new house. They often stayed with their grandparents in the holidays so that Dad could work, but it felt like the trip hadn't ended yesterday when they came home. Everything was still strange, even though they'd spent a night at the new house before going away and had been allowed to pick their own bedrooms. Abby now had to creep across the house to wake Chris in the mornings, but that hadn't stopped her today.

'Do you think they deserve the surprise?' Dad asked, with a look that was every bit as naughty as any his daughter could assume. 'I'm sure there are some better behaved kids who are much more deserving, probably on this street.'

'Dad,' said Abby, furious in that special way of hers. 'We are deserving! And you have to love us, it's the rules.'

'I always love you, even when you're a monster,' he replied with a smile.

'Can we have some cereal?' Chris asked quietly.

'Of course,' Mum said. 'Get your sister some and then, once you're dressed, you can play outside while some of us go to work.'

Chris set about getting breakfast, with Abby helping, as Mum made herself some toast and marmalade to eat with a cup of tea. Dad put his cup in the sink and gave her a hug.

'I'm still not sure it was a good idea,' Mum said quietly.

'What else were we going to do with that bit of the garden?' he asked.

'I know, but you're the writer. It's the start of a very good horror story and the vendors were awfully glad we bought this house.'

'The house had been on the market for years and the commute was exhausting for them,' Dad said, with a laugh.

'It just feels weird,' said Mum seriously.

'It will be fine, Claire, you wait and see. They're going to love it.'

'Love what?' asked Chris, who was eating his

Chapter 1

cornflakes while Abby munched away at her chocolate cereal, delighting in the changing colour of her milk.

'You'll see,' said Dad, with a tired wink. 'I'm going to grab a shower before your mum goes to work.' He walked out of the room, running his hand through his messy hair and yawning theatrically.

'Can I get down?' Abby asked, having drunk the last of her chocolate milk directly from the bowl.

'Go get dressed.'

'Is everything okay, Mum?' asked Chris. He'd been listening to his parents while Abby focused on her breakfast.

'You shouldn't listen in on other people's conversations, young man.' Mum's telling-off was half hearted. 'I'm fine, just a little tired. I know everything is strange but you'll get used to it here and I think you'll love what we've done in the garden.'

'Thanks, Mum. Can I get down now?'

'Of course. Go get dressed and clean your teeth. Make sure your sister does the same.'

Chris carefully put Abby's and his breakfast dishes in the sink then rushed upstairs to his room. He closed the door behind him and looked round; everything was put away neatly but he could soon sort that out. He put on his favourite T-shirt, a Sheffield Wednesday football shirt, and his shorts and trainers.

He wondered what the surprise was; hopefully it would take his sister's mind off her tree at the old house. He knew she missed that tree more than anything, even though it was diseased and Mum had shouted at her for climbing it when she'd been told not to. He was confused by what his parents had been talking about, but adults were always having strange conversations about things that didn't make sense.

He left his room and knocked on Abby's door.

'What do you want?' Abby shouted.

'Mum says we need to clean our teeth,' said Chris and, with the order passed on, he went to the bathroom.

Dad opened the door as Chris approached; his brown hair was still damp from the shower and even more of an unruly mess than usual. He was a tall man, even by adult standards, and broad and hairy like some kind of alien.

'Hey, Chris.' Dad smiled at his son and gave him a conspiratorial wink. 'Hurry up and get ready so we can look at the garden before your mum leaves for work.'

'I've just got to clean my teeth like Mum said.'

'Good lad.' Dad ruffled Chris's hair and headed for his daughter's room. 'Come on, monster, clean your teeth so we can take a look at your surprise.'

Abby shot out of the door, hugged her dad's leg enthusiastically and bolted for the bathroom, running and turning a cartwheel as she went past the top of the stairs.

'Abigail Arwen Cromwell,' her mother called crossly. 'What have I told you about messing about at the top of the stairs?'

'Sorry, Mum.' Abby instantly slowed to a walk and went into the bathroom to clean her teeth.

Chris watched his mum and dad share an exasperated look and then followed Abby, wondering what the surprise would be.

CHAPTER 2

The Surprise in the Garden

'Three, two, one, open,' said Mum and Dad in unison.

They had made Abby and Chris close their eyes in the kitchen and then led them into the garden. The grass was still damp with early morning dew as they walked across it unsteadily before being brought to a stop. When she opened her eyes, Abby jumped for joy and ran towards the open door of a shed in front of a tree, where her tea set was carefully laid out on a small table. A selection of her toys were sitting around it.

Chris looked up at his parents with a huge smile. 'Thanks,' he said. 'Do you have time to play?'

'Sorry, Chris, but I've already missed this deadline so I have to work. But I'll play with you soon, I promise,' Dad replied.

'Okay,' said Chris, failing to hide his disappointment. He turned to the goal posts and training cones that were laid out on the lawn and soon forgot to feel sad.

'I've got to go, kids,' said Mum. 'But have fun and be good for Dad. He's got a lot to do.'

Abby sprinted back to hug Mum, who crouched down and gave her a big kiss. As Abby turned back to the shed, she noticed the swing hanging from the tree behind their shed for the first time. 'That's brilliant, Mum,' Abby called, as she ran straight to the tree and scampered up the trunk like a monkey.

'I really have lots to do, Chris, so I'm putting you in charge,' Dad said. 'I'll be able to see you from my office. If you two behave yourselves, we'll have toasted sandwiches for lunch.'

'Okay, Dad.'

* * *

The morning passed quickly. Chris dribbled his football round the cones and ran drills that he'd learnt on a football skills course earlier in the summer holidays. Abby spent most of her time clambering round her new tree, going higher and higher.

'Abby, come down,' Chris shouted. He was getting worried.

'Why?'

'You're very high. If you fall, you could really hurt yourself.'

'No, I wouldn't – I'd be dead and wouldn't feel a thing,' his sister replied in a sing-song voice.

Chris couldn't remember being seven very clearly, but he was sure that he hadn't said as many strange things as Abby did. He had once heard a teacher call Abby a 'macabre little girl'; he didn't know what macabre meant, but guessed it wasn't nice or the teacher wouldn't have looked so embarrassed when he had asked her.

It was amazing what adults would say when they thought you weren't listening and, ever since he had read a book about spying, Chris liked to listen carefully. He

Chapter 2

also tried to memorise all the cars on his street, which was another trick from the same book, but he always got them muddled up. He could name all sorts of obscure footballers but cars were boring.

'Abby, please,' he tried again. 'I'd be really sad if you hurt yourself.'

'Sorry, Chris.' Abby eased herself down the tree a little.

'What have you got in the shed?' Chris asked, looking back at the house. His dad was sitting at his desk, buried in his work.

'I'll show you!' Abby suddenly dropped out of the tree and started to run. 'Come on!'

Chris followed her into the shed. The door was in the middle of the side facing the house and had windows on either side. Directly opposite the door, near the back wall, was the low table where Abby's toys were seated on chairs, taking tea. To the left of the table was a toy oven. Finally there was a low workbench and a couple of stools so you could sit and colour in or play board games. There was a pair of wooden shelves against the left-hand wall; one had books on it and the other was stacked with boxes of games. To the right of the door was a box with their rugby ball and frisbee in it, and behind that were their bikes.

'Wow,' Chris said to Abby, who was sitting on one of the bean bags in front of the bookshelves. 'This is cool.'

'Yep,' she agreed.

Chris noticed that as well as board games there were jigsaws, science sets and a box of magic tricks. Most of the books were about things to make and do. Chris selected a book about card tricks. He settled down on the other bean bag, looked at his sister for a moment and began to read.

'So I take it you guys approve,' Dad said from the doorway of the shed.

'Yes,' Abby and Chris chorused.

'So much so that you don't want lunch?'

'Daddy,' said an exasperated Abby. 'You promised us toasted sandwiches.'

'If you were good! But it appears you have been, so come into the kitchen.'

Lunch was really tasty: ham and cheese toasties with salad and tomatoes, followed by tinned peaches. Dad even let them have lemonade.

Their dad still hadn't finished his work, so in the afternoon Chris had to play football with Abby. Once she got bored, they threw the frisbee and set a new record of sixty-four throws, before finally playing snakes and ladders. Finally Abby decided that she wanted to draw and, having found reams of paper and her art things in the cupboards under the workbench, she contentedly set about drawing the shed and her new tree.

Chris went outside to play football some more and was busy scoring the goals that would get Sheffield Wednesday promoted when Mum called from the back door, 'Dinner in ten minutes, guys. Time to pack up.'

'Mum,' whined Abby from their shed.

'Time to pack up and wash your hands,' said Mum firmly.

Chris picked up his cones and ball and put them back in the shed. Abby straightened up her things and they

Chapter 2

trooped back to the kitchen.

'I drew these for you.' Abby thrust three pictures into Mum's hand before heading to the sink to wash her hands.

'Thank you, Abby. Let's see, you've drawn the shed, the tree with your swing and... What's this?'

'That's the rabbit that lives in our shed. It was really hard to draw because when he came up through the floor he was just a skellington. But then he grew insides and muscles and eyes and fur so he looked like a normal rabbit. I tried to draw that happening but I don't think it came out right.'

'That's ... impressive,' Dad said, standing in the doorway with an odd expression on his face. 'I'm not sure I would know how to draw that either.'

'There's no rabbit in the shed,' Chris exclaimed. 'I would have noticed.'

'There is too! He just likes me better than you. He was hiding while you were in there and only came out when you were kicking your stupid ball again.'

'Now, kids,' said Dad. 'You nearly managed a whole day without being monsters.'

'Thanks for the goalpost, Dad,' said Chris, feeling just a little sad. 'It's brilliant.'

'I'm glad you like it.' Mum smiled. 'Now wash your hands or no dinner.'

Mum and Dad were quiet over dinner and kept exchanging glances but Abby and Chris didn't notice as they were focused on the important matter of food.

'Please can I get down?' Abby asked when she had finished.

'Yes, it's bath time. I'll be up in a minute,' said Mum.

'We'll do the washing up,' Dad offered. 'It's about time Chris worked on his drying up.'

'But Dad…'

'I don't *have* to let you play on your console tomorrow,' said Dad with a theatrical wink. 'In my day…'

'Okay, I'll help.' Chris hurried to the sink, not wanting to hear the rest of the speech.

Chris had his bath after they finished washing up and, because he was really tired, went to bed early and hardly read any of his book before falling fast asleep.

Downstairs, Mum and Dad sat with a cup of tea. 'That's some imagination your daughter's got,' Mum said.

'I don't know where she gets these things from.'

'You don't think there's anything to what she said?'

'Claire, I just wish I had her imagination. Perhaps I wouldn't be in so much trouble with my editors.'

But Mum was not so sure that everything was as it seemed.

CHAPTER 3

A Scream in the Afternoon

The next few days were the kind of hot lazy summer ones that grandparents tell you don't exist anymore. Abby and Chris were happy playing outside in their new garden and playhouse. Abby found a new branch for balancing on and spent as much time up her tree as in the playhouse. Chris was working hard on his left-footed shooting, and had begun practising card tricks from what he now thought of as 'his' book.

Abby had only mentioned the rabbit once more but then stopped talking about him to Chris because her brother stubbornly refused to see anything. Dad was still spending most of his time bent over his laptop or with his nose in a book; with each passing day Mum got a little crosser with him because he still hadn't finished his work.

That afternoon, Chris caught the ball beautifully with the laces of his left boot and blasted it into the top right-hand corner of the goal. He ran to the goal, grabbed the ball, set it back in the same position and tried again. His aim wasn't as good this time, but it still hit the top corner and he was pretty happy with his efforts.

He was making a third attempt when he heard a shocked scream from inside the playhouse. He ran round the shed to the doorway and found Abby looking at the back corner.

'Bad kitty! You put Fluffy down right now. Don't shake him by the neck, you bad cat,' she finished furiously, taking a step forward.

'Abby,' said Chris hesitantly. 'There's nothing there.'

'You put him down,' Abby continued, ignoring Chris. Then she stopped and giggled. 'You two were playing! I thought you were hurting him.' She turned and smiled. 'It's okay, they're just playing.'

'Who are?'

'My rabbit Fluffy and this cat. I haven't given her a name yet because she's only just come to play.'

'There's nothing there,' Chris said crossly. 'Stop messing about.'

'There is too! It's not my fault you're too stupid to see them,' Abby shouted. She bent down to pick up her imaginary rabbit and stroked it behind the ears. 'Now go away. We don't want you here.'

'Abby—'

'Go away!'

Chris knew his sister too well to argue, so he went back to playing football but his heart wasn't in it anymore. He went back into the house.

'Is everything okay?' Dad shouted from his office.

'Abby is pretending that her imaginary pets are real,' replied Chris. 'And she called me stupid.'

'Why did she call you stupid?' Dad asked, walking into the kitchen and ruffling Chris's hair.

Chapter 3

'I told her there was nothing there,' Chris said reluctantly, looking at his black and yellow football trainers.

'You had imaginary friends at that age too, you know. It's a normal part of growing up.'

'But…'

'What, Chris?'

'I don't know,' Chris said, kicking at his heel. 'Do you want to play football?'

'One game,' said Dad. 'I'm nearly finished and it'll be a good break – but go easy on your old dad.'

'I will,' lied Chris, as competitive eleven year olds do.

* * *

Chris only beat Dad 5–1 and was slightly grumpy about the goal that he conceded, but he was getting better at controlling his frustration these days. He went to the kitchen to get some water when Dad went back to work. From the way Dad bounced along the hallway, it looked like he'd almost finished his book.

As he drank his water, Chris looked out of the kitchen window. His sister was dancing along one of the branches of her tree. It was an old oak with a thick trunk that split into a number of broad branches, several of which reached down to the ground. Now that Chris thought about it, the tree didn't really belong in the garden: it was too big and too old. Who would have planted something like that? Chris didn't know how old the house was, but he knew that trees grew slowly so the tree must be a lot older than the house.

The garden was now baking in the mid-afternoon sun.

Abby hung from one of the tree branches and then dropped onto her swing. Chris started practising keepy-uppies but the heat got worse and eventually he walked to the shed, which was shaded by the tree, and sat on a bean bag. Slowly he drifted off and was daydreaming of scoring goals and starting at a new school when Abby walked in. He heard her muttering but he couldn't be bothered to open his eyes.

'Come here, Tabitha,' muttered Abby.

Chris awoke with a start as the strangest sensation of ice-cold fur brushing against his bare leg made his skin crawl. He glanced around in shock but there was nothing to see.

'Well, now you've woken him up, Tabitha. I hope you're happy.'

'What?' asked a confused Chris.

'Sorry, Chris. Tabitha didn't mean it, she was playing.'

'Who is Tabatha?' Chris sat up and rubbed his eyes.

'My cat.' Abby pointed at a space in front of Chris as if it was the most obvious thing in the world.

Before Chris could reply, there was a knock at the door. 'Can I come in, kids?'

'No,' replied Abby, giggling.

'Come in, Dad,' said Chris hopefully. 'Have you finished?'

'Yes, I have. Do you guys want to go to the village shop and get an ice cream to celebrate?' Dad ducked as he walked into the shed and crouching to hug Abby.

'Yes,' the children chorused.

'Come on, then,' Dad smiled and watched as Chris and Abby pushed past him and shot across the lawn.

Chapter 3

Dad trailed behind them and, having grabbed his wallet from the hall, led them down the road. They were walking back from the shop, each of them licking their lollies when they met a pair of old women not far from their house.

'Hello, dears,' said one of the women with a warm smile. 'Enjoying your ice creams?'

'Yes, thank you,' Abby replied primly, instantly deciding that she liked the strangers.

'Hello,' said Dad. 'I'm Tony. I don't think we've met.'

'Yes, we saw the removal vans. My name is Daphne and this is my friend Nora.' Daphne pointed at her friend who looked quite stern and who merely nodded hello.

Daphne had lots of grey curls framing her friendly face and warm smile. Her brown eyes were bright and she had a beautiful carpet bag of many colours. Nora was dressed in a dark skirt and grey blouse, with a pair of steel reading glasses hanging from a chain round her neck. Her iron-grey hair was cut shorter than Chris's and she had cold green eyes that seemed to be watching Abby very carefully.

'Do you live on the street?' Dad asked.

'We live just down there, dear,' Daphne said. 'Are you settling in?'

'Getting there. You know how it is.' Dad smiled.

'Well, if you need to know anything about the area or someone to watch the children then please ask.'

'Thank you,' Dad replied.

'We should be going, Daphne.' Nora sounded as if she was worried her friend would stand and chat all day. 'Or we'll be late.'

'Oh, ah ... yes.' Daphne beamed at everyone. 'Enjoy your ice creams.' And with that, the two old ladies walked off towards the village.

Abby headed straight back to the house but Chris stood and watched them for a moment.

'You okay, chief?' Dad asked.

'Did you see the way the stern one was looking at Abby?'

'Not really. And if we don't hurry, your sister will have trashed the house and Mum will never forgive us.'

'Dad,' said Chris hesitantly as they started to walk back to the house.

'Yes?'

Chris wanted to tell his Dad that there was something odd about the two old ladies, and there was something else he couldn't remember, but looking up at his dad he faltered. 'Can we play some football?' he asked, not sure why he didn't want to talk about what was worrying him.

'Almost certainly. I've got to make a phone call now that I've sent in my first draft but after that there should be time.'

'Dad, will you ever write something I can read?'

'Maybe one day. I've just never thought of anything that you would *like* to read.'

CHAPTER 4

Tea with Strangers

Dad cooked one of his curries that night, pretty much using every pan in the process, but it was really tasty and Mum looked relieved that she didn't have to cook. Chris, Abby and Dad had played football for a bit but Dad's phone call seemed to have taken forever.

'They want me to go to London,' Dad said, as they ate their food.

'When?' asked Mum.

'Next week. The publishers want to see me and my agent is up to things.' He pulled a funny face.

'Like keeping you in work,' Mum laughed.

'Can we come too?' asked Abby excitedly. 'I want to see the dinosaurs.'

'There wouldn't be time,' Dad said sadly. 'I'm afraid I'll have lots of boring meetings with adults talking about boring things.'

'Being a grown up is rubbish,' said Abby.

'Sometimes it is,' said Mum thoughtfully. 'We'll talk about it later.'

After dinner Mum took Abby upstairs for a bath and Chris helped with the washing up, although he wasn't allowed to handle the sharp knives. It seemed to take forever and they still hadn't finished when Mum came back so she helped while Abby sat at the table and started drawing, singing to herself.

'So what do we do with these two?' Mum asked quietly.

'I don't know, although...' Dad said thoughtfully.

'What?'

'Well, we met a couple of old women from across the road this afternoon who offered to babysit if we needed them to.'

'So you want to leave our kids with strangers?' Mum asked. 'Old ones who probably couldn't keep up with our two monsters.'

Chris kept quiet throughout this exchange; for some reason he was quite scared of having to answer to the stern old woman he'd met earlier.

'Why don't we invite them over for tea and you can meet them? Even if you think it's a bad idea to leave the kids with them, inviting them in would be neighbourly. We've been so busy we haven't met anyone yet.'

'That's not a bad idea,' Mum said reluctantly. 'They might not be able to help next week but it would be good to see the neighbours. I'll stop by tomorrow morning while you look after this pair.'

* * *

Saturday morning cartoons were the best. Abby and Chris sat watching the TV while their parents slept upstairs. 'I'm hungry,' Abby whined when the programme they were watching finished. She skipped towards the

Chapter 4

door.

Chris followed his sister to the kitchen, 'Why don't you sit down and I'll get you some cereal?' said Chris.

'I want to do it,' Abby said crossly. 'I can get my own cereal. I can do anything you can.'

'Okay, okay.' Chris watched as Abby dragged a chair across the kitchen so she could stand on it and get her cereal out of the cupboard. She put the box on the table before dragging the chair towards the fridge.

'What's all this?' asked Dad from the kitchen door way. 'Are you trying to break our lovely new tiles, Abby?'

'No,' laughed Abby. 'I wanted breakfast.'

'And Chris couldn't have got it for you?'

'I can do anything he can,' Abby repeated.

'Yes, you can,' said Dad. 'But sometimes you have to wait until you've caught him up in size or age.'

'That's not fair.'

'Yes, it is,' insisted Chris, who had noticed that Abby was allowed to do things when he was and didn't have to wait until she was the same age.

'Enough you two.' Dad smiled. 'I'm here so *I'll* get the breakfast.'

'But...'

'That's the rules,' said Dad solemnly to Abby, cutting off her complaint. He made everyone breakfast while Mum had her Saturday morning lie-in. They were two-thirds of the way through the food when suddenly Chris flinched. The ice cream and Dad's celebration yesterday had distracted him, but he suddenly remembered the other thing that had worried him as he once more felt ice-cold fur against his shin. When he looked down there was nothing there, but he saw his pyjama trousers move as something nuzzled against his leg.

'Are you alright, Chris?' Dad asked.

'Tabitha surprised him,' Abby said.

'Tabitha?'

'My ghost cat.'

'Chris?'

'Sorry, Dad,' said Chris. 'I...'

There was a moment's pause and Dad said, 'Very funny, kids,' and laughed at what he thought was a joke. And with that, Chris felt he couldn't say anymore.

* * *

Mum got up later and invited Daphne and Nora for tea that afternoon. After lunch she shooed the kids into the garden with a smile and a promise of cakes if they didn't make a mess of the house.

Abby sat in her tree, playing with a couple of dolls and singing to herself. Chris went into their shed and started to rebuild some of his old Lego kits. He was confused by what had happened to him, but felt silly talking to his parents about something he couldn't show them. He was distracted for a while as he tried to reassemble the gear box from his car kit without the instructions, and he was deep in thought when it struck him. What if there was something in one of their books?

He dropped his misaligned gears and hurried to the bookshelf but, after a careful check of the books, he had to concede that there was nothing that would help him.

'What are you doing?' Abby asked.

'Looking for a book,' replied Chris.

'Can I help?'

Chapter 4

'No, we don't have what I wanted. Do you want to play something?' Chris tried to distract her, not wanting Abby to ask what he was looking for.

'Chris, Abby,' called Mum from the kitchen door. 'Come here, kids.'

Chris and Abby trooped into the kitchen to find Daphne and Nora at the kitchen table drinking tea. The table had a shop-bought cake on it, but there was also a plastic box that contained some delicious-smelling home-made scones.

'Hello, dears,' said Daphne, with a warm smile. 'Would you like a scone?'

'Yes, please,' Abby replied. 'Can I have some juice, please, Mum?'

'Of course. Do you want some juice as well, Chris?'

'Yes, please,' Chris said, making a point of going and sitting by his dad. 'And can I have some cake?'

When they were sitting round the table, Chris noticed that Nora did not eat any cake but took small sips of black tea. Once again she watched Abby carefully, although no one else seemed to notice.

'Are you enjoying the holidays?' Daphne asked the children. 'We've had lovely weather for you to be out in.'

'My new tree is even better than my old one,' Abby said happily round a mouthful of scone, spraying the table and her juice with crumbs.

'Abby!' said Mum, exasperated. 'You know better than that.'

Chris looked at Dad and both of them worked hard to stifle a laugh that would get them into trouble, although there was the hint of a smile on Mum's face. Nora continued to look very serious.

'Sorry,' Abby said, having finally swallowed her food.

'Why is it *your* tree?' asked Daphne.

'It's got my swing and I get to climb it. And it likes me – I hear it whispering in the wind.'

'That sounds lovely. Would you like to show me when we've finished eating?' Daphne sounded genuinely interested.

'Okay,' said Abby, before taking another bite of her scone.

'I sometimes think Abby spends more time off the ground than on it,' said Dad. 'But I'm probably just jealous.'

Chris watched as Dad, Mum and Daphne laughed at Dad's joke but he wasn't sure why.

'I take it that's your goal,' Daphne said to Chris.

'I like to play football too,' Abby interrupted before Chris could answer. 'But he's much better than I am.'

'Only because he practises so much,' Mum said.

'You like football a lot?' Daphne asked Chris.

'Yes,' Chris replied. There was something incredibly comforting about Daphne; it felt like she could be a nan to everyone in the world and would look after anyone who needed it. She chatted happily as if she had been a family friend for years.

Soon everyone was full of tea and cake. Chris was feeling a little bit sleepy, but there was still a bright glint in Daphne's eyes. 'Can I see your tree now?' she asked Abby.

'Okay.' Abby got up and led the old woman to the door.

CHAPTER 5

The Garden after Tea

Chris watched as Abby walked hand in hand with Daphne across the grass to the tree. He followed them on to the lawn but jogged over to his goal and started to practise his ball-juggling at an angle where he could keep a suspicious eye on the pair of them. Mum and Dad set about washing up, occasionally glancing out of the window to check on their children. Nora planted herself in one of the garden chairs on the patio by the back door; she checked on her friend and the girl for a moment before settling down to observe the boy watching them.

'Daphne's lovely,' said Mum, rinsing off a plate and placing it in the rack.

'She's as talkative as Nora is stern,' Dad commented thoughtfully.

'Having second thoughts?'

'It was never a serious plan,' Dad said defensively.

'It would get us out of a bind on Monday while I sort out an alternative.' Mum placed another plate in the rack and turned to look at her husband. 'And it could be a useful arrangement. You can never have too many child-care options.'

'That's true.' Dad leaned down and kissed Mum on the forehead. 'But we do seem to have swapped roles.'

Mum didn't seem to notice that comment and turned back to the washing up as Dad started working out what he needed to pack for his trip to London.

* * *

Nora stood up and walked briskly over to where the boy was juggling the ball. As the ball fell out of the air, it seem to swerve unexpectedly in a slight breeze so Chris's foot caught it just a fraction away from where he wanted and it flew in the wrong direction, away from his sister and the old woman.

'Do you always keep such a close an eye on your sister?' Nora asked as she approached.

Chris waited a moment before turning to reply. As he did, out the corner of his eye he saw Daphne reach down and scratch the air absent-mindedly, as if fussing an affectionate cat.

'Dad says one of the important things about being a big brother is looking out for your sister.'

'Does he?' Nora studied Chris carefully. 'So you would be eleven, yes?' Chris nodded. 'You will be going to a different school to your sister. Who will look out for her then?'

'There will be teachers and her friends. She'll be okay.'

Nora nodded approvingly and changed the subject. 'Do boys your age still climb trees or do you spend all of your time playing video games?'

'I'm not as good at climbing as Abby but it's fun.'

Chapter 5

'But not Abby's tree?' Nora asked casually.

Chris was about to answer when he was interrupted.

'Nora dear, have you seen this plant,' Daphne called, before turning to Abby. 'Why don't you play with your brother while Nora and I discuss plants?'

'Can't I look at the flowers too?' Abby asked.

'It's not a flower, dear, and it might be poisonous. Can you please play with your brother while we check?' She bent down to scoop up their frisbee and handed it to Abby.

'Okay,' Abby said, nodding seriously. 'Let's break the record, Chris,' she called, running towards him and throwing the frisbee enthusiastically. The throw was not a good one. Abby was off balance so the frisbee veered off course and whistled past Chris. For a moment it looked like it was going to hit Nora on the nose but, just as Abby was about to call out in warning, Nora plucked the flying disc out of the air with one hand.

'I think you need to be a bit more careful if you want to break any records,' Nora said sternly to Abby as she handed the frisbee to Chris and joined Daphne.

As Chris and Abby started their game, the two old women walked further into the garden. Daphne could barely suppress the spring in her step. 'A potential witch, after all these years!'

'The girl clearly has a warrior's soul,' Nora said quietly.

'She has got herself a spirit familiar without any training. We can't just dismiss a ghost cat.'

'I'm not, Daphne, but use your head. Was there ever a witch with a warrior's soul who didn't turn bad in the end?'

'But she's a good girl…' Daphne stopped by a neglected flower bed and bent to inspect a weed.

'We'll have to keep an eye on her but we can't train her. You know that.'

'I know,' said Daphne reluctantly. 'It's just been so long and it would be nice to have the company.'

'You'd take that girl from her brother and parents?'

'No.'

'Well, then. We'll keep an eye on them. We can't have spirits wandering around the place willy-nilly. Besides, she might not be the only one with potential.'

'Christopher?' asked Daphne, surprised. 'There hasn't been a warlock since…'

'Since Merlin, and history called him a wizard or druid. But the boy has something about him.'

'Does he now?' Daphne smiled broadly as she straightened up. 'And you'd take that boy from his family?'

'I didn't say that,' Nora snapped. 'But he has talent. He saw you fussing that damn cat, even as I tried to distract him.'

'Oh,' said Daphne sheepishly, understanding the rebuke.

'I know you were bonding with the girl but the boy was watching you. He knew something was up, even if he couldn't see anything.'

'So the boy doesn't actually have powers,' Daphne said triumphantly. 'Only you could think of teaching someone magic because they had a good head on their shoulders.' Daphne turned to look at the children. She didn't know what Nora was up to but she had an inkling.

'If we'd had a few more with some common sense, we wouldn't be in this mess, would we?' Nora said bitterly.

'It might have helped.' Daphne nodded her head towards the house. 'As would a few more with powers.'

'The time of magic is finished,' Nora said firmly. 'Our job now is to make sure that any remnants of that time are dealt with safely.'

'We'll keep an eye on the children for the next few days,' Daphne muttered under her breath as they approached Chris and Abby. 'I'll take care of the parents.'

'I started the process while you were with the girl but I'll let you finish it.'

'Thank you.' Daphne suppressed a smile. That was as close as she would get to Nora admitting that Daphne was better at something than her. 'You know the boy is still young enough for his power to manifest.'

'I hadn't forgotten,' said Nora sharply.

Abby heard her new friend Daphne and the other old lady approach and turned to call to them as Chris made his next throw of the frisbee. 'Were the plants poisonous?'

As the words left her mouth, there was a gust of wind and the frisbee sailed overhead and flew into Abby's tree. The two old ladies exchange a sharp glance and Daphne walked over to Abby.

'No, dear, they were a type of weed that looks a bit like a poisonous plant. Now, shall we speak to your mum about you helping me bake on Monday?'

'That'd be brilliant,' said Abby excitedly, trotting after Daphne back to the house.

'You'd better get that frisbee,' Nora said to Chris.

'Abby's gone,' he replied, frustrated. 'And we were

going to break the record.'

'There'll always be another day,' said Nora. 'But you go get it and then we'll work out what we're going to do with you tomorrow.'

'Okay,' said Chris.

He ran over to Abby's tree and shinned up the trunk, swinging up into the branches and grabbing the bright yellow disk. He dropped the frisbee to the floor, dangled, then dropped out of the tree. When he was on the ground again, he picked up the frisbee and ran to Nora.

She nodded approvingly when he stopped in front of her. 'Now, young man, if you don't mind being dragged away from the kitchen, I could do with a hand in the garden tomorrow.'

'Okay,' Chris said, without much enthusiasm.

'I could do it myself but a younger back will make shorter work of it. And then maybe I can show you my workshop.'

'Okay.' Chris yawned.

'Let's get you back to your parents. You'll be no good to me if you're half asleep.'

* * *

Chris followed Nora back to the house. After the old women had gone he sat on the couch, exhausted, while Mum and Dad tidied up. They sent him to bed early that night, promising that it wasn't a punishment but just that he seemed to need it. Chris would have argued about it being unfair but he was too tired and went to bed without protest. That night he slept very soundly indeed.

CHAPTER 6

The Cottage and the Impossible Garden

Chris spent most of Sunday dozing but woke up Monday morning feeling rested, although he still ached all over as if he'd been stretched in every direction. He half expected to have grown over the past day but when he checked himself in the mirror, he looked no different.

Chris had been up for barely five minutes before Dad was hugging him and Abby and getting into a taxi to leave for his trip. Mum rushed them through breakfast, made them brush their teeth and get dressed, and soon they were marching down the road to Daphne and Nora's house. The old women lived in a cottage that seemed out of place on the street; it looked as though the various houses around it had popped up like unwanted guests.

They pushed open the small gate in the overgrown hedge and emerged into a quaint little garden with a well-kept lawn and flower beds that were exploding with colour. 'It's so pretty,' Abby said, clearly awestruck.

'What must they have thought of our garden?' Mum whispered to herself.

Abby skipped down the path to a weathered green door set in bright, whitewashed walls. Mum and Chris followed. Daphne had already opened the door by the time they caught up.

'Good morning, dears,' she said brightly. 'Would you like a cup of tea?'

'I've got to get off to work,' Mum said sadly. 'But maybe this evening. And thank you so much for helping with the kids. Now, you guys, be good!' She crouched down and kissed Abby, gave Chris a quick squeeze and then walked away. Abby looked startled to have been left so abruptly and Chris thought it was odd because they'd never been here before. He laid a reassuring hand on Abby's shoulder as Daphne welcomed them in.

'Come on, you two. Have you had breakfast?'

'Yes, thank you,' Chris replied. Abby had gone uncharacteristically quiet.

The children walked hand in hand into the strange house, which was dark and cool. They could see very little as the door shut behind them with a heavy thud, cutting out the light.

Daphne squeezed past and led them down a short hallway. She opened a door into the kitchen which was dominated by a large wooden table. Nora was sitting there, finishing off some dry toast and sipping at a large cup of tea. 'Come in, you two,' she said.

'They've had some breakfast,' said Daphne. 'But I think they should have a glass of milk before we start working them.'

Chris was about to protest but Daphne continued enthusiastically, 'You have to try some of our goat's milk. It's fresh, Nora just milked the goats.'

'You have goats!' Abby cried, suddenly coming out of

Chapter 6

her shell.

'It would be hard to milk them if we didn't,' said Nora, almost – but not quite – smiling.

'You can meet them later.' Daphne went to a cupboard and produced two glasses. 'Sit down, dears.'

Chris and Abby sat down facing Nora. The kitchen smelt of freshly baked bread and was warm in contrast to the cool hallway. Daphne set two glasses of milk in front of the children and Abby stared nervously at them. Chris looked at his sister and then at Nora, who gave him a curt nod, but it was Daphne's encouraging smile that made him reach forward and take a cautious sip. The milk was chilled, creamy, rich and delicious, despite sending a strange shiver from his stomach to the rest of his body. After that first wave of cold, he felt suddenly refreshed.

'It's delicious,' he said, taking a longer sip. 'Thank you.'

Abby paused for a second then also started to drink, smiling broadly as she hurriedly finished her glass.

'Right.' Nora stood up. 'Chris and I have things to do.'

'Okay,' Chris said. 'You'll be okay, Abby?'

'We're going to bake,' Abby said happily.

'I'll take good care of her,' Daphne promised. 'You'll have some lovely cakes for tea this afternoon.'

Nora looked at Chris as he got up. 'We'll have to change your shoes. There should be something suitable in the shed.'

'Okay,' said Chris, looking at his orange and yellow football trainers. He followed Nora out of the back door and into the garden. There was another lawn and some flower beds; at the back there appeared to be a gap in the hedge that surrounded the garden. There was a small shed just in front of them but Chris couldn't see anywhere to keep goats.

'Let's get you some proper boots.' Nora fumbled in her pocket and produced a large brass key with which she unlocked the shed. She stepped inside and started rummaging but Chris couldn't see what she was doing, 'These should fit,' she said finally, turning and holding out a pair of stout-looking wellies and some thick socks.

Chris sat on the kitchen doorstep to put them on. The socks were incredibly warm and soft and the wellies had protective toecaps and fitted perfectly. He put his trainers in the kitchen next to several other pairs of shoes and took one last look at his sister, who was following Daphne around the kitchen asking questions.

'Come on, Chris,' Nora said. 'This way.'

Chris turned to see Nora striding quickly across the lawn and followed. Looking at the surrounding houses, he could not understand where they were going. It looked like the hedge was pressed up against the back fence of a modern house that loomed over the garden. Nora didn't even break stride as she confidently walked through the gap in the hedge, but when Chris reached it he paused.

'Come on then,' barked Nora impatiently. 'We've lots to do today.'

Chris looked round him, feeling that he was going a little mad. However, he seemed to have little choice so he stepped into the small gap, pushing between the branches of the hedge, expecting to walk into a very solid fence at any moment. When he stepped out of the hedge into an extension of the garden, he gasped in surprise.

Chapter 6

The hidden part of the garden stretched before him. Chris was standing on a path that led between well-kept vegetable beds to a stone outhouse with a thatched roof. To the left, beyond the vegetable beds, was a large enclosure where three goats nibbled at some overhanging vegetation from the forest beyond. The forest stretched around them in a wide arc, as if the cottage and grounds occupied a clearing in the middle of it.

'Come on then, lad.' Nora was already walking towards the shed.

'But...' Chris said in confusion, before running after the old woman.

They arrived at the outhouse. Nora opened a cupboard on the outside of it and handed Chris a hoe and fork. 'I need you to clear these two nearest beds,' she said. 'We're resting them this year but I don't want the weeds to get out of hand. I'm too old to clear them myself.'

'But...'

'Oh, don't worry, everything in those two beds can go. Once you're used to the work, I'll show you what needs to go in the other beds.'

'That wasn't what I was going to ask.' Chris finally found his voice. 'What is going on? Where are the other houses?'

'Where we left them,' Nora said sharply.

'But they've vanished.'

'Don't be absurd, Christopher Cromwell. Houses don't just vanish.'

'But they're not there.' Chris pointed at the trees. 'We should be in the garden of the house behind your cottage and yet somehow we're stuck out here in the middle of a forest.'

'Very good.' Nora watched Chris thoughtfully. 'Of course, I *could* just explain but what would that teach you? So I suggest you have a good think about it as you work on the veg beds. Exercise is an excellent way of helping you think things through. It gets the blood flowing to all the right places.'

'I...' But Chris didn't know what to ask, so he hefted the tools he'd been given and walked to the first bed. Nora showed him how to use the hoe and he set about clearing his first vegetable bed, all the while trying to work out what was going on.

CHAPTER 7

Work and More Questions

The morning passed quickly. Chris found himself enjoying the work as he slowly piled up the weeds in an old wheelbarrow and carried them to one of Nora's monstrous compost heaps. He watched her when he could and she seemed to be very capable as she pottered round the garden, tidying up and weeding. Given how hard he was working, though, it made sense that she wanted a younger person to clear the rested beds. What would she have done if Chris hadn't been there? He gave this plenty of thought but he didn't have any real idea. The only explanation he had for where they were seemed so unlikely that he discounted it.

'Time for lunch,' Nora said. She had walked across to Chris without him noticing.

He surveyed the morning's work and was surprised to see that he was about two-thirds of the way through clearing the beds. Now that he'd stopped, he was suddenly so hungry his stomach started growling.

'I think someone is ready for their lunch,' Nora said.

'Yeah,' Chris laughed. 'I guess so.'

'Come on, let's see what Daphne has been up to in the

kitchen.'

Chris followed Nora back down the path to the cottage. As he approached the hedge he had an idea and paused for a moment when he reached the gap. He tried to look to his left as he walked through the gap, hoping to see what happened to the houses that should be surrounding the cottage. Despite trying to hold his head up, however, several overgrown branches and the spiked stem of a bramble forced him to drop his gaze. By the time he could look up again, he was standing in the cottage's back garden. He turned and stared at the houses that once again overlooked the garden.

'Hmm.' Nora nodded in approval as Chris faced her, then she stomped to the back door.

'Take your boots off, dear,' called Daphne cheerfully as Chris arrived at the kitchen door.

Chris eased his feet out of his boots and walked across the tiled floor to take a seat at the kitchen table. The air was thick with delicious smells. Abby seemed to be covered in flour but she was beaming happily.

'Wash your hands,' Nora said quietly, after Chris sat down.

Chris got up to wash his hands and Abby gave him a friendly shove as she went to her chair. Soon he was sitting opposite Abby, with Nora sat at one end of the table while Daphne fussed around them. She produced a plate full of cheese and ham, a huge bowl of salad and a home-baked loaf of bread that was still warm to the touch.

'I helped make that,' Abby said proudly.

'Yes, you did.' Daphne finally sat down. 'And I'm sure

Chapter 7

these two are going to be grateful for it. How's the garden?'

'Coming along,' Nora replied.

'I bet Chris has been a great help. You two, help yourselves.'

'He'll do,' said Nora, slicing a thick wedge of bread.

Quiet soon descended on the table as everyone tucked hungrily into their lunch. The food was delicious and Chris soon felt energised again and ready for the afternoon's work. He sipped some cool water that tasted better than anything he had drunk before and watched Abby finish her food. 'Have you had a good morning, Abby?'

'Yes, I have. We baked and Daphne told me about yeast and kneading dough, although my hands were too small…'

'I told her she wouldn't have to wait long,' Daphne laughed. 'But patience doesn't come easy at her age.'

'Why can't we just be as big as we want to be?' asked Abby. 'Then you wouldn't have to say "wait until you're bigger".'

'One day you'll understand,' Daphne said.

Chris wondered why adults always said things like that; he guessed hearing it was part of growing up.

'As these two cooked, we'll do the washing up,' Nora said to him. 'And then we need to get on.'

Nora washed the lunch things and Chris dried them, including the sharp cheese knife. Nora made sure he was careful with it and told him it was important that he learnt responsibility. They were soon back in the hidden garden, the hedge once more defeating Chris when he tried to see where they were going.

He had got the hang of the gardening and, although it was hard work that seemed to take a long time, he soon cleared the second bed. He looked up and found that Nora was watching him.

'How are you doing, young man?'

'It's hard work,' said Chris honestly, looking at his watch. 'What else do we need to do? Will we have time to get everything done?'

'We'll get back in time,' said Nora. 'But I think you have done enough. You might have to help me turn the soil in the autumn when we're digging in the compost but it's too early for that now.'

'I could do that,' Chris said enthusiastically; he had enjoyed his first foray into gardening.

'Come on then,' said Nora. 'Let's put those tools away. We still have things to do.'

Chris followed Nora to the outside cupboard and passed her the tools. She wiped off any dirt and placed them back in the cupboard. Then she said, 'Follow me,' and opened the outhouse door with another large brass key. 'Follow me,' she said again as she opened it.

Chris stepped into a single room. The air was heavy with the scent of herbs drying in bunches hanging from beams, and a large table stood in front of him covered with tools. To his right was a large set of shelves filled with jars. He felt that he didn't want to look too carefully at the contents of those jars, so he wandered round the other side of the table and looked at the open fireplace.

'Grab one of those baskets,' said Nora, pointing to the table. 'We have some work to do in the woods.'

Chapter 7

Chris picked up the wicker basket, which held a small fork and a trowel, and followed Nora as she led him into the forest.

The forest was like nothing he had been in before. There was no wide path for them to follow; instead they picked their way along a small track that wound through the trees. At regular intervals Nora stopped to inspect a tree or small plant, occasionally squeezing, smelling or tasting parts of the plants and occasionally using a pair of secateurs to cut leaves or flowers from them. The trees seemed to lean further over them as they went deeper into the forest and Chris was glad he had a guide. On his own, he would have been lost in seconds.

'Here we are, Chris.' Nora stopped in front of some trees that seemed to be spaced further apart and were surrounded by rows of low-growing plants with red berries. There was a compost heap nearby. 'We need to check these rows for any weeds and pull them up.'

'Are you sure we'll be back in time for Mum?' Chris asked anxiously. 'There's a lot of plants to check.'

'We'll be fine. Let me show you what we're looking for.'

They worked side by side, pulling up the weeds and checking for pest damage. The plants were in excellent condition but it took quite a while to check them all and the sun was shining through the trees at a low angle by the time they finished.

Suddenly Chris looked up, sure he was being watched. He stared hard into the trees, looking for a pair of eyes, but if there was someone or something there it was too well hidden for him to spot.

'I've got one last thing to show you,' said Nora, before walking off into the woods. 'You can leave the basket by the compost heap. We'll pick it up again on the way back.'

CHAPTER 8

Revelations and Mysteries

As they walked further into the woods, Chris still had a nagging sensation of being watched, but there seemed to be no one in the forest except for Nora and him so he tried to ignore it. They didn't walk for long before they came to a clearing. Chris stopped in surprise at the edge while Nora strode confidently into a stone circle in the centre of the clearing.

'Enter the circle, Christopher Aragorn Cromwell,' Nora commanded.

Chris's feet obeyed even before he had a chance to think about it. He found himself in front of Nora, staring into her green eyes as she muttered something to herself. He turned to look at the stones and saw that the forest was alive with glinting eyes hidden amongst the trees. The circle was protecting him and Nora from whatever had been following them. A shiver ran through his body, and he gasped as a tingling sensation swept through his brain.

'You're safe for now,' Nora said.

'What's going on?' replied Chris, trying to swallow his fear.

'We haven't seen a potential witch in nearly a century, and now we have one playing with spirits in their back garden.'

'I don't understand what you're talking about. What are those things out there?' Chris asked. He could feel the interest of the strange creatures pressing against him and somehow he knew they were not human.

'They are of no concern.' Nora's hand suddenly shot out and grabbed Chris's shoulder in a vice-like grip. A stab of pain drove him to his knees and he felt Nora looking at him as he slipped into a darkness filled with whispers in languages he didn't understand.

* * *

'Come on, Chris or we'll be late for tea,' said Nora, pointing at the door.

Chris set down the basket of cuttings from the forest and left the outhouse. Back at the cottage, he took off his boots by the door. He walked into the kitchen yawning; he ached in the way you do when a day's work out of doors is behind you.

'Hello, Chris dear,' Daphne said. 'Looks like you've been hard at it.'

'Yeah, there was a lot to do.'

'We've been working hard too.' Abby pointed at the table which was laden with sandwiches, scones and cakes together with pieces of fruit and a large teapot.

'Mum will be here in a minute,' Abby said. 'Is Nora okay?'

'I'm fine, thank you,' said Nora sharply as she appeared behind Chris at the back door. For a moment she looked

Chapter 8

exhausted before she pulled herself together.

'You two sit down and rest,' said Daphne, a flash of concern crossing her face. 'I hope you haven't been overdoing it.'

Chris looked at Nora but she refused to show any more weakness and went to the deep kitchen sink to wash her hands. At Nora's command, Chris went to wash his hands too. As he did so, there was a knock on the front door

'Mum,' cheered Abby, who shot down the hall with Daphne trailing behind her.

'Hi, Chris. Goodness, what a spread,' Mum said as she came into the kitchen.

'Look what we made,' Abby said proudly.

'I thought you might like to take the evening off cooking,' said Daphne. 'Have a seat and I'll get you a cup of tea. Help yourself to food.'

'That's very kind of you. Thank you.' Mum sat down heavily on one of the kitchen chairs and looked around. 'So, have you two been behaving yourselves?'

'Yes,' Abby replied. 'I helped make the bread!'

'Wow, that's great love,' said Mum as she took a couple of sandwiches. 'Thank you, Daphne.'

'She's been no trouble,' replied Daphne.

'And you Chris?' Mum watched her son tuck ravenously into a large plate of food.

'He's been helping me in the garden,' Nora said. 'He worked very hard.'

'Did you enjoy that?' asked Mum.

Chris nodded. When his mouth was empty, he exclaimed, 'Yes! Could we have veg patch at home?'

'We'll talk to Dad about it when he gets back.'

They soon settled down to their food. The children talked about their day and Daphne chatted brightly; Nora sat quietly watching them as she wearily ate a sandwich and a plain scone. Finally they tried the cupcakes that Abby had made with Daphne while Nora ate slices of apple.

'Don't you want a cake?' Abby asked sadly.

'Nora has to be careful how much cake she eats,' said Daphne. 'I think she's saving her cupcake for something special.'

'That's right,' said Nora. 'But they look … lovely.'

Chris smiled to himself as he watched Nora trying to find a word to describe the cake that would please a seven-year-old girl. He could tell that eating sweet things was not something she did, rather than something she disliked. He asked, 'Do you have diabetes?'

'Something like that,' Nora replied. 'When you get to my age, you have to be careful what you eat.'

'How old are you?' Abby demanded.

'Abigail Cromwell!' Mum protested.

'I'm as old as my hair and a little older than my teeth,' Nora said sternly. Daphne and Abby giggled.

Mum stood up. 'I ought to get these monsters home. They need to get ready for bed.'

'Awww,' Abby whined, but Chris was ready to go.

'So,' said Daphne, 'we'll come over to your house tomorrow if that's alright? Then Chris and Abby will have their things to play with and that huge garden to run around in.'

'Your garden is so pretty.' Mum tried to hide her

Chapter 8

embarrassment about the state of their own.

'It's easy when you have the time,' Nora said.

'Say goodnight,' prompted Mum to her children.

'Goodnight,' Chris and Abby chorused.

They followed Mum down the hall and Daphne ushered them out. 'See you tomorrow,' she called as she shut the door behind them.

As they walked down the path, Chris looked at his watch and couldn't believe how late it was. Where had the time gone?

* * *

Daphne walked back into the kitchen to a cupboard where she pulled down a large jar filled with a mixture of tea, herbs and other more secret ingredients.

'You can drop the act now, Nora Jane. I've known you for too long,' said Daphne, frowning as she started to make a very different kind of tea.

Nora allowed her shoulders to sink a little, but there wasn't much change in her bearing.

'So what happened?' Daphne asked.

'The boy has power,' said Nora, allowing tiredness to seep into her voice. 'I took him to the circle and naturally we were followed.'

'How many?'

'Not so many that holding a protective circle did this,' said Nora wearily. 'But the ritual with Chris was hard.'

'You went too deep looking for any magic?' asked Daphne as she let the tea brew.

'No, I had to contain *his* magic so we didn't attract unwanted attention. I haven't felt anything like it before.

The moment he crossed into the stone circle... I have never seen or heard of such a transformation. He went from a boy with no talent to containing all the power of a fully-trained warlock. I'm not sure Merlin himself had access to such reserves of magic.'

'What?' Daphne exclaimed, horrified. 'Anything with an ounce of magical skill left would be interested enough in a potential witch, but if they've got that strong a signature to look for then how are we going to protect the boy or his sister?' Daphne trailed off and turned to pour the tea, busying herself with strainer and cup until she had collected herself.

'It's all right, Daphne. I managed to contain the power between the two of us within the circle. Even the eyes watching us don't know what happened.'

'I didn't think that was possible.' Daphne set down Nora's tea and took a seat next to her friend.

'Only when they're young,' said Nora. 'You know what a stickler Auld Alice was for the theory.'

'You were the one who was trained by her. She was just a legend by the time I learnt anything of magic.'

'She told me herself about the technique, although she had never used it. You can use a potential witch or warlock's nature to block their own power. Due to their age and lack of training, it's difficult for magic to pass through a young witch's body. It's part of what makes using magic in the early days so difficult and unpleasant.'

'I remember even the simplest of spells made me feel sick for days,' Daphne said with a shudder.

'Quite. Well you can use that difficulty to slow the flow of magic through them, particularly if they are

Chapter 8

unconscious. Then you take control of their mind and use it to direct the flow.'

'But such an intrusion is a forbidden practice.' Daphne couldn't hide her horror at what her friend had said.

'If it was anyone other than an untrained potential witch, it would be an intrusion of the most unforgivable kind. But as Chris and Abby have not developed the senses to feel what happened, they are completely unaware. Or so I hope.'

'You hope?'

'I have never attempted this before,' said Nora quietly. 'When could I? Neither of us were witches long enough to have apprentices before the magical lands were separated because of the peace agreements. Anyway, the boy passed out. I did what I had to, then altered his memory to stop him from being suspicious.'

'We'll have to tell him soon, if that kind of power is awakening in him,' said Daphne, watching her friend carefully.

'We will have to tell both of them,' replied Nora, sipping at her restorative tea.

CHAPTER 9

A New Friend

Chris was stiff and sore when he woke up the next morning. His joints ached and he had a tingling numb sensation from his big toe, through his foot, round the side of his ankle and up to the inside of his knee.

He sat up in bed and tried to ease the tightness in his shoulders and neck. When he put on his watch, he had to correct the time as it seemed to have gained a couple of hours. When he climbed out of bed his legs gave way for a moment. He stumbled across the room, trying to get used to the strange feeling in his lower legs, then went across the landing past his sister's empty room.

Chris could hear voices in the kitchen as he made his way carefully downstairs. He went into the kitchen and found Mum getting ready leave to leave, Abby eating breakfast and Daphne and Nora sitting at the table, sipping tea.

'Good morning, dear,' said Daphne. 'Are you a little sore from gardening yesterday?'

'Yes,' replied Chris as he made his way awkwardly to the kitchen table.

'Have a seat,' Nora said crisply.

Chapter 9

'We brought you some fresh milk.' Daphne poured some of their goat's milk into a glass and passed it to Chris.

'Thank you,' he said, taking the glass and drinking from it automatically. It was just as delicious as yesterday and once more a cold shiver started in his stomach and swept through his body. Suddenly he felt a little better. He drank the rest of the milk quickly and the adults watched him with amused smiles.

'I think someone needed that,' said Mum, as Daphne refilled Chris's glass. 'I must get going. Have a good day, kids.'

Abby jumped up and gave her mum a big hug. 'Have a good day, Mum.'

'I will. Now, you two behave yourselves.'

'We will,' Chris and Abby chorused.

They all followed Mum down the hall and waved her off to work.

'Would you like some breakfast, Chris?' Daphne asked.

'Yes, please.' Chris walked stiffly back to the kitchen and drank his second glass of milk as Daphne poured him some cereal. It wasn't until he was half way through the bowl of cereal and goat's milk that Chris realised that Daphne seemed to know her way round their kitchen. He didn't know why this bothered him but it did.

'Can we do some more baking?' asked Abby.

'Maybe this afternoon,' Daphne said. 'But I'd need to find everything first. Why don't you make the most of this beautiful day.'

'But you need to clean your teeth first,' Nora ordered.

'Awww,' replied Abby, but the look she got from Nora cut off any further complaint. 'Okay. Can I get down now?'

'If you're finished,' said Nora.

'Thank you for breakfast.' Abby skipped out of the kitchen and Chris heard her run up the stairs to get dressed.

Chris finished his breakfast in companionable silence with the old women. When Abby came back down, she shot straight out into the garden.

'Will you help me with the washing up?' asked Daphne.

'Okay.' Daphne washed the dishes as Chris dried and Nora watched Abby. Chris looked out of the window and saw his sister shin up her tree and start exploring. She was dancing along her balancing branch as he dried a bowl. There was a cat prowling along the top of the shed as Abby walked and twirled.

After Chris got dressed and cleaned his teeth, he felt a little better but he was still tired so he went to the playhouse to be by himself and work on palming a coin. His practice didn't go well and it was very frustrating. His fingers seemed too clumsy to manoeuvre the coin and he kept dropping it. The next time it fell to the ground, he was too slow to stop it rolling away.

He was trying to see where it was when he heard a strange noise, a scratching sound behind him. He looked around but the sound was definitely coming from below, at the back of the shed. He walked out of the door, waving cheerfully at the two old ladies who were sitting by the kitchen door. He held his breath but they stayed where

Chapter 9

they were as he made his way round the shed and passed out of sight. He wasn't sure why, but he was sure they were hiding something.

'What are you looking for?' Abby called, dangling from her tree and watching her brother investigate the back of their shed.

'I heard scratching.' Chris crouched down but he couldn't hear anything. Maybe he had imagined the noise.

Abby dropped out of her tree ran over. 'Let me see.'

They listened but Chris couldn't hear anything and he turned away.

'There's something there,' Abby said confidently. 'Chris, you need to call him.'

'Call who, Abby?' asked Chris, looking at his sister in confusion.

Abby laughed. 'Your dog, silly. Go on, he's looking for you.'

'There's nothing there,' Chris said crossly but then he felt a horrible freezing cold pass through him, sending a shiver to his core. From nowhere, a cat landed in front of him and walked over to Abby who tickled its ears.

'Abby, your cat!' Chris said in shock. 'I can see your cat.'

'Hello, Tabitha, did you frighten Chris?'

'She just jumped through me.' Chris stared at the pale ghost cat that was nuzzling his sister. He looked at them for a moment and then called gently, 'Here, Dog. Come on boy.'

'You'll have to try harder than that.' Nora appeared from around the shed and made both Abby and Chris jump.

'But...' All Chris got from Nora was a hard stare so he turned back to the shed. He listened carefully and could just make out a frantic scrabble of claws from underneath the shed. Reaching out with all his will, he called, 'Come on, Dog. Here, boy.'

There was plaintive woof from beneath the shed and more scrabbling, accompanied by a series of barks. Suddenly a pale ghost dog sprang out of the ground in the front of them, bouncing up and down in front of Chris and turning circles as he barked enthusiastically.

'A cocker spaniel,' said Daphne. 'How lovely.'

'What is going on?' Chris wondered if he was going mad. He turned in exasperation to the dog and told it firmly to sit, which the shaggy and long-eared ghost promptly did.

'Why on earth should we know?' Daphne replied with an amused smile.

'But we'll find out,' said Nora darkly.

'How?' asked Abby.

'Let's sit out in the sun and we'll talk about it.' Daphne looked up at Abby's old oak tree before making her way back towards the house.

Chris turned to Abby, who shrugged and followed the old ladies across the lawn with Tabitha in tow. He looked at the ghost dog, who was panting and staring at him eagerly. 'Come on then,' he said. Dog scampered around Chris's legs; every time he passed through a part of Chris's body the boy felt a stabbing sharp cold in his legs.

'Sit down, dear,' Daphne said to Chris.

Chris looked at the ghost dog, who seemed to have taken a dislike to Tabitha and was watching the cat very carefully.

CHAPTER 10

Explanations and a Warning from History

'So what's going on?' asked Chris, sitting on the grass facing the old ladies.

'I told you, we don't know.' A hint of frustration crept into Daphne's voice.

'Have you seen many ghosts?' Abby asked quietly, looking fondly at her cat.

'Not for many years,' Daphne replied sadly.

'Who are you?' asked Chris.

'Just two old women who know a thing or two.' Daphne gave him a kind smile.

Chris stared at them, his mind racing. He looked at Nora. 'The question is not *where* your garden is but *when*?'

'Very good.' Nora gave an approving nod. 'Although you've been a little slow.'

'Are you witches?' Abby asked.

Daphne laughed loudly and even Nora looked amused, but it was Daphne who took up the story.

'For a long time we never really had a name, my dear. We were simply the wise women for the village, but witch is as good a name as any. Some of us who remained were called witches, but then some witches were just old ladies who knew more than men wanted them to. Sadly they were burnt at the stake...'

'Daphne,' Nora said sharply. 'Please start at the beginning.'

Daphne looked startled, 'Why don't you tell them then? It's too sad...'

But Nora didn't seem to know how to start either so they sat in silence until Abby announced, 'It's like *Horrible Histories*.'

'We know about witches and the witch trials,' said Chris, nodding in agreement. 'We've heard about them.'

'But you don't know everything. There was once magic in the world,' Nora said sadly. 'Magic was a resource, like coal or oil, and like any other resource it requires management and careful use. One day you might learn the full history but, for now, it is enough to say that there was a great war between the different magical races. It was like any other war, except that because magic was involved there was a possibility that someone could destroy the world completely. As things began to get desperate an alliance was formed that led to a peace treaty. The magical lands were separated and, where necessary, as much magic as possible was removed from some of those lands, including ours.'

'But you're witches. Don't you need magic?' Chris asked, looking at the two ghost pets.

'Barely any trace of it is left here,' Daphne said.

'And what remains has to be watched carefully. That's where we come in,' Nora explained. 'There are a few of us left who are the guardians of the accord, the agreement to govern the use of magic and its interaction between

Chapter 10

the various lands.'

'So ghosts are magic?' asked Chris, looking at the two ghost animals and wondering what else there might be.

'Not usually.' Daphne took up the story. 'Ghosts are just spirits that haven't moved on or have been disturbed in their rest. They are a type of memory. They shouldn't have a form or shape.'

'It takes power to give them a body, even one as fragile as these, and there is so little magic left.' Nora looked at the children sitting between their ghost pets. 'If it was just a couple of animal spirits that would not be a problem, but magic attracts magic these days. In such quiet times, even the slightest whisper can be heard for miles around. We don't yet understand how the pair of you have managed this.'

'Us?' asked Abby.

'In our day, children like you would have been taught to use their skills. Not everyone who has the talent for magic can learn the craft, but a *potential* witch was usually someone that could do great things.'

'Or terrible things,' Nora added.

'What do you mean?' Chris asked. 'We didn't do anything?'

'Except somehow you have spirit animals as pets. We call them "familiars".' Daphne smiled.

'But...'

'Yes?' Nora asked.

'I don't understand,' Chris finished.

'As I said, neither do we,' replied Daphne. 'For now this is our secret.'

'We shouldn't have secrets like this from Mummy.'

Abby looked scared. 'Should we, Chris?'

Chris didn't know what to say. Part of him wanted to tell Mum, but for some reason he trusted these old women – or at least he trusted their intentions.

'You can tell her,' said Daphne, showing some of the steel hidden behind her fluffy old woman facade. 'But I will make sure that she won't believe you. I would rather save the magic in case we need it for something else. We could be facing a great danger, but that will not stop me if you do not keep this secret with us.'

Chris knew that they were not telling him and Abby everything but he also knew he had to make a decision. 'It's okay, Abby. We know these witches now. They know magic but Mum and Dad don't. If they say it is safer for only us to know, then we have to trust them for now.'

'That's settled then,' said Nora, watching Chris carefully.

'For now,' Chris repeated with emphasis, meeting Nora's gaze. He was surprised when she looked away.

* * *

The rest of the day passed in a strange haze. Abby baked with Daphne in the afternoon and Chris tried to distract himself by playing football. There had been more goat's milk with lunch and he had drunk some tea with Nora and Daphne afterwards. He felt much better now and was strangely aware of his own body; his left foot no longer felt like a stranger with a mind of its own. With a little concentration, he could do the same things with it that he could with his right foot. He had just completed twenty keepy-uppies using only his left foot when Nora

Chapter 10

approached him.

'You don't trust me young man.'

Although distracted, Chris kept the ball in the air with his right foot, settled it on his head for a moment before flicking it up and volleying it into the top corner of his goal. He turned to face the old woman.

'Very impressive,' she said.

'Thank you.'

'We have a problem.' She stared at him.

'We have a problem or *you* do?' asked Chris.

'We,' said Nora firmly. 'It might have started with familiars, which used to be something of a rite of passage for a witch in training. Or warlock,' she added with a slight nod of recognition. 'But the kind of power that is giving your pets a shape and form will attract attention – and not just from friendly animal spirits.'

'How do we know the animals are friendly?' Chris asked.

'Woof,' barked Dog, who had spent the whole day trailing Chris and was now lying by the goal, wagging his tail.

'Well, there's your answer. Although you can never tell with cats,' Nora said with a frown.

'Should I be worried?' Chris was beginning to fret about his sister.

'Yes, but not about the cat. Daphne tells me that all of the pets have appeared near the shed.'

'I suppose they have,' said Chris. 'But you'd have to check with Abby to be certain.'

'We're going to take you back to our house tomorrow until we can find out what is happening. Until then, keep away from your shed.'

'Why?' asked Chris, turning to face what looked like a perfectly ordinary building.

'The spirits have appeared there for a reason,' replied Nora. 'But even if we work out why there, that doesn't explain how they are taking form. There has to be a vein of magic somewhere.'

'A vein?'

'Untapped magic, like a vein of gold in a mine. Or maybe worse,' Nora said.

'Worse?'

'I didn't want to have this conversation in front of Abby.' Nora stepped forward and stood close to Chris. 'When I was a girl, this kind of thing was common but there was proper magic then. Not like now. If there is a vein or source of magic then Daphne and I should be able to sense it, but neither of us can find anything. Perhaps we're missing something or we are too rusty but I think not. There is something else out there. I know that telling the pair of you not to play with these spirits won't work but, believe me, the more contact you have with them, the more likely you are to attract the attention of other things.' Nora laid a heavy hand on Chris's shoulder.

'Like what?' asked Chris, the memory of eyes in a forest flashing through his mind.

'Hard to say exactly, but almost certainly something you would rather not meet.'

'Is magic bad?' Chris asked, wondering why almost everything he had been told was a warning.

Nora seemed to lift a weight off his shoulders when she removed her hand. 'In of itself, no. But power is

Chapter 10

always dangerous, especially when the source of that power is scarce. People will do very bad things to each other for power, and even worse when they are scared or desperate. The war was…'

'What?'

'Too difficult to explain.' Nora looked sternly at Chris. 'And not because you are too young but because I don't know how to explain. What you see here is the result of a long, terrible struggle. Daphne and I … there are so few of us left now and our powers are merely shadows of what they once were. Maybe you will get to see.'

'What could we see?' asked Chris, still remembering his distrust of the old women.

'If you are lucky, the state of the world before history was re-written.'

'Who re-wrote it?'

'We did,' said Nora darkly. 'For its own good.'

CHAPTER 11

A Walk in the Forest

Nora seemed reluctant to talk any longer and avoided further attempts to continue their conversation. Then Mum came home and the old women left, but not before sitting down to a meal with all of them. Chris slept that night with Dog lying at the foot of his bed, guarding him.

Chris had done his best not to fuss the animal but Dog had followed him around loyally all evening, keeping out of everyone's way while keeping a watchful eye over his new master. Chris didn't know how he was meant to avoid the ghosts if they followed them everywhere. Tabitha seemed to treat everyone except Abby with disdain; even then, Tabitha only tolerated short periods of fuss from his sister before she wandered off to do whatever a ghost cat did when it was out of sight. At least Fluffy the rabbit seemed to be happy living in their shed

While they were eating breakfast the next morning, there was a knock at the front door and Mum went to answer it.

'Hello, dear. We thought we'd pick up the children and take them for a walk this morning,' Daphne said brightly.

Chapter 11

'That sounds lovely. Come in. I've got a lot to do today. Would it be okay if I left you with them now?' Mum asked, looking at her watch.

'Of course you can,' said Daphne, and Mum rushed off to get ready and leave the house.

'You will need some sturdy shoes,' said Nora, eyeing Dog carefully. 'We don't want you getting sore feet.'

'Where are we going?' asked Abby.

'I think you'll enjoy it.' Daphne winked. 'Now finish your breakfast, we have lots planned for today.'

The children finished their breakfast in record time and Chris had some tea with Nora while Daphne helped Abby pick a suitable outfit for walking.

'So where are we going?' asked Chris curiously.

'Woof,' barked Dog, earning him another interested look from Nora.

'Just round the local countryside.'

Chris looked carefully at Nora. 'This is some kind of test, isn't it?'

'Almost everything is,' she said, with what passed as a smile for Nora.

Once they were ready, Daphne and Nora led the children out through the front door followed by Tabitha and Dog. When they reached the pavement, both ghost animals stopped.

'Aren't you coming, Tabitha?' Abby asked but the cat seemed to shake its head and stalked back towards the house.

'Come on, Abby.' Daphne took Abby's hand. 'You'll see her later. You can't make a cat do anything it doesn't want to.'

Chris watched as the cat faded away then looked down at Dog, who was lying at the end of garden as if he was prepared to wait all day for Chris's return.

'Come on, lad,' Nora said, and they walked down the street towards the old ladies' cottage.

Daphne led them down the front path before turning off across the grass and down the side of the cottage.

'We'll have to do something about their shoes,' said Nora, walking towards their small shed. 'Come on, children.' She unlocked the door and disappeared into the shed. Considering how small it was, she seemed to spend a long time inside. When she reappeared she was holding a pair of walking boots with some thick socks stuck inside them. 'Here you are, Chris,' she said. 'And these are for you, Abby.' She held out another pair of walking boots.

Abby loved them. 'Thank you,' she said, taking the bright yellow boots with a smile. 'They're pretty.'

They were soon ready to go. 'Let's go, then,' said Daphne, and led them to the gap in hedge at the back of the garden.

'Everyone hold hands,' Nora said. Chris looked at her questioningly. Her hand felt ice cold as it engulfed his, in contrast to Abby's small warm hand that he was also holding.

Nora stepped into the gap with everyone linked together. She looked back and gave a small nod to Daphne. Then there was a strange squeezing sensation and they walked into a clearing in a wood.

'Wow,' said Abby, dropping Chris's hand and turning around as Daphne let go of her.

Chapter 11

'You like it then?' Daphne was clearly amused by Abby's reaction.

Over the treetops Chris could see a mountain that shouldn't be there. He looked quizzically at Nora as Abby started skipping and cartwheeling round the clearing.

'Go on then, Chris,' Nora said quietly.

'Is this a "where are we?"' asked Chris.

'Where and when, lad,' said Nora. 'I'll explain once we're moving.'

'Is it safe?'

'That's why we're here,' Nora replied approvingly.

Daphne walked confidently to the start of a half-hidden path. It was unlike any path Chris had seen before; this was no cleared space created by someone, and yet the plants seemed to have agreed where they should walk. And walk they did, enjoying the forest.

'So where are we?' Chris asked Nora as Abby skipped ahead looking at the strange flowers, Daphne telling her their names.

'Hard to say exactly. The scientists are getting better but even I get lost when they start talking about different dimensions. We are in another world would be the easiest way to say it.'

'But...' Chris said. He had so many questions he didn't know where to start.

'Take a minute, we've got plenty of time,' said Nora, recognising Chris's confusion.

'How?' asked Chris. 'How are we here?'

'There's a knack to it. Not everything we do is magic and, in this case, it suits our purposes as there is no magic in this particular world.'

'You said magic wasn't evil so why are we avoiding it by going somewhere else.'

'We're not the only thing that can travel across worlds. Magic can pass through the tiniest of cracks and travel between worlds, all the while remembering how it was used. We need to do some tests without any other source of magic confusing things. And we want to keep you two a secret.'

'Is that why the ghosts stayed at home?' asked Chris, looking round. Some part of him expected to hear a faint woof.

'No, they couldn't have followed us here. Whatever magic has given them form is tied to something near your house and so they have to stay near it.'

'Why is there no magic here?' asked Chris. 'If magic can squeeze through cracks and remember then why isn't it here?'

'I don't know.'

'You and Daphne say that a lot,' Chris challenged.

'It's better than lying to you. The way I understand it, there are too many possibilities to count. By stepping across here, we passed from where our home is to a world where magic doesn't exist, or not in a form we recognise. I was shown how to get here by someone smarter than me who told me not to go exploring unless I didn't mind dying. There are more dangerous worlds out there, paths to other planets. You don't want to walk to the moon or step into an ocean and drown. I don't fancy exploring too much and we've got a peace to keep, so it is a mystery I choose to accept.'

'It's like a computer game with loads of different

levels,' Chris said, looking sharply at Nora, 'And each level is a different type of game, but some levels will kill you straight away if you go there.'

'I don't go in for computer games much, but that's not a bad way to put it. However, this game only gives you one life and you can only play it once.'

'Are you coming?' shouted Abby, sounding surprisingly far away. 'I've found a brilliant tree.'

'So why are we here?' Chris asked.

'Because we wanted a nice walk.'

'And?' Chris had the feeling that Nora was enjoying being challenged.

'Well, it doesn't hurt that you can't play with those pets while you're here,' Nora replied sternly. 'Now, come on, the others will be fretting.'

Nora and Chris had to walk a long way down the path to catch up. Daphne was standing beneath a strange tree that Abby had shinned up with her usual skill. The little girl was now doing handstands with her feet resting against a parallel branch.

'It's brilliant here,' she shouted cheerfully, but Chris wasn't so sure.

CHAPTER 12

Missing Hours and a Return to the Garden

They walked for hours in the forest and Chris's misgivings slowly subsided. Nothing bad happened as they wandered among the beautiful trees. Daphne seemed to know the name of every plant or flower and happily shared them with Abby and Chris, while Nora followed them with a satisfied look on her face.

The trees started to thin and then a huge grass plain opened up before them. There was a steep hill to their right. 'Follow me,' said Nora, starting to walk up the hill.

'Race you to the top.' Abby broke into a run.

'I'll still beat you,' called Chris, chasing after his sister.

The two of them were about half way up the slope when the race finished without a winner as they were too tired to run. They both stood looking at the view as they tried to catch their breath.

'You can see for miles,' panted Chris. Abby nodded, too tired to speak.

'Come on you two,' said Daphne brightly as she and Nora strode past. 'Slow and steady wins the race.'

The view from the top of the hill was worth the effort. Behind them the forest stretched on to meet the sky and

Chapter 12

in front the land fell away to the sea.

'Where are we?' Abby asked. 'How do we get home?'

'Good questions,' said Daphne. 'You three stand over there.'

'Chris?' asked Abby, but her brother didn't have an answer and only shook his head in response.

Daphne reached into her multi-coloured carpet bag and pulled out a jar of earth. 'Abby and I will go first.'

'Go where?' Chris asked as Abby took a step towards her brother.

'Home, lad,' said Nora.

'How?'

'Magic,' replied Nora.

'But...'

'Not now. Let your sister go and then I'll explain,' Nora interrupted.

'B...'

'In a minute.'

'Would you like to do some magic, Abby?' Daphne asked.

'Can I?' asked Abby, looking scared but excited at the same time.

'Come here.' Daphne beckoned Abby to her.

Abby looked at Chris for a second then walked to Daphne. 'What do I do?'

'Pour this earth around us in a circle. There must be no breaks in it.' Abby poured the earth carefully until they were surrounded. 'Now pass the jar to me and hold my hand,' said Daphne.

Abby handed the jar to Daphne, who threw it out of the circle to Nora and then waved her hand. A slight shimmer appeared round the circle; Daphne whispered something under her breath and she and Abby vanished.

'Abby,' shouted Chris, panicked by her disappearance. 'Where did they go?'

'I told you, home,' Nora said shortly.

'Is Abby okay?'

'Don't be absurd, Christopher Cromwell. Of course she is.'

Nora's tone of voice and the use of his full name made Chris turn to face her. 'Could you please explain what is going on?'

'This is a test. We have deliberately brought you to a land with no natural magic and asked you to try a simple transportation spell using the earth in this jar as the source of power for the spell.'

'But how do I know you're telling the truth?' asked Chris. The jar of earth seemed completely ordinary to him. 'How do you know that Abby is okay?'

'Because this is a controlled test. At worst, the magic won't flow through you and nothing happens. If it does, then an experienced magic practitioner is performing a simple spell. As Daphne and Abby are quite clearly not here, the spell worked. Your sister is perfectly safe. If you would be so kind to as to pour your own circle of earth then we can get back to your sister and put your mind to rest.'

'Fine,' Chris answered grumpily, snatching the jar of earth that Nora held out to him and walking in a tight circle round the pair of them. As he closed the jar, Nora laid a hand on his shoulder. For a second it felt as if someone was pouring water into one ear and making it

Chapter 12

flow out of the other. Chris shook his head and realised that he was standing in Nora's vegetable garden in the middle of a shower of rain.

'Into the workshop,' said Nora. 'Let's get out of this rain.'

They ran to the outbuilding and Nora unlocked the door so they could get inside. She went straight to the fireplace and quickly lit a fire. 'Time for tea, I think,' she said. 'How are you feeling?'

'Cold and hungry.'

'No nausea? You're a natural.' Nora took down an old kettle and filled it from a water pump in the corner of the workshop. 'Lucky you. I felt sick for hours the first time I did a spell.'

'Got the kettle on, Nora?' Daphne asked, walking into the workshop and shaking her umbrella. 'Come on, Abby.'

Abby followed, looking distinctly unwell. Daphne ushered her to a stool near the fireplace. Abby was shivering and there was a sheen of sweat on her forehead.

'Is she okay?' Chris asked.

'Nothing that a cup of tea and a spell by the fire won't fix.' Daphne gave a reassuring smile. 'I could barely stand after my first time.'

'Nora said she felt sick.'

'And all *he* feels is hungry.' Nora opened a cupboard and retrieved a teapot and some mugs.

'Well,' Daphne laughed, 'I've got just the thing to help with that.' She produced a tin of biscuits, offered one to Abby and then took one for herself.

Soon they were all holding steaming mugs of tea and

munching biscuits – except for Abby, who still felt sick.

'So why are we cold in the middle of summer?' Chris asked, looking at the damp garden shining under a blue sky.

Daphne sipped her tea. 'The spell we cast uses a magic circle to create a link between worlds. When using this link, you have to cross the void between the worlds and that's as cold as anything can be. Drop yourself in the Sahara and you'd still feel the chill from it.'

'Not to mention that the sudden change in temperature would kill you,' muttered Nora.

'I'm not sure I like magic,' Abby said, slurping some of her milky tea.

'That's okay, dear. You don't have to perform any. We just needed to confirm that you could and that's why you can see the ghosts. No one will force you to do any magic.'

'Has that always been true?' asked Chris.

'No,' said Nora. 'In our day, if you showed a talent for magic you would be trained. But ours was a time of magic and it was considered a great privilege to be one of the wise, or a witch, so no one would dream of refusing. I'm not sure how useful the craft would be to you these days. You must trust us. Despite what you have seen over the last few days, there really is very little magic left since the peace treaty was put in place.'

'So what do we do?' asked Chris.

'Daphne and Abby can make some lunch while I show you a couple of things in here. After we've eaten, we'll do some gardening this afternoon.'

'Sounds like a plan to me,' replied Daphne.

Chapter 12

'Can I help with the garden?' Abby asked, putting down her mug and munching on her first biscuit.

'Of course.' Nora nodded approvingly.

* * *

Chris and Nora stood in silence as Daphne and Abby walked back to the cottage. When they disappeared from sight, Nora asked, 'You had some more questions?'

Chris looked at his feet for a moment. 'What if I wanted to learn the craft? Could I?'

Nora looked at him sadly. 'It's not that simple. It isn't something you can dabble in. It takes all your effort to master the craft of magic and you don't have time because you have to go to school.'

'But...' Chris looked at his watch. 'Hold on. My watch was wrong the other day. What time is it?'

'Very good,' said Nora. 'Lunchtime. Time moves at different speeds in other worlds but that won't help you.'

'But we could make time,' Chris said excitedly.

'No, I'm afraid we can't.' Nora shook her head. 'I'm not sure which of the various theories of time is right, if any of them, but time past is time passed to the person experiencing it. If you came to this garden to spend an extra two hours learning magic, that would still make your day two hours longer, even if you stepped straight back into your world right after you left. The hours would add up, you would need extra sleep, and you would age too quickly. What matters is the time you *experience*.'

'But what about you and Daphne? You go everywhere and talk as if you have lived centuries.'

'A very good question.'

CHAPTER 13

A New Visitor

Chris did not sleep well that night. Nora had tried to answer his question but Chris could only follow a little of what she scribbled on the blackboard. In the end, all her explanations reminded him of the Doctor on TV saying wibbly-wobbly timey-wimey... stuff.

He was still dozing, with Dog lying quietly at the end of his bed, when Abby sneaked into his room. 'Are you awake?' she asked.

'Yes. What's up, Abby?'

'I'm scared, Chris.'

'What of?' Chris sat up and rubbed his eyes. Dog let out a reproachful whine as Chris sat up, pulling his blanket through the translucent body of his pet ghost. 'Sorry, Dog.'

'I don't like all this magic.'

'You like Tabitha though,' said Chris, as Dog gave Abby a reproachful stare.

'And Dog.' Abby scratched the ghost between his cold ears.

'Do you like Daphne and Nora?'

'I think so. Nora can be a bit scary but I liked gardening.'

Chapter 13

'I don't think we're going to do more spells any time soon, so I think you should be okay. Is there something else that's worrying you?'

'Why don't they know what's going on?'

'Adults don't know everything. Usually they pretend to but Daphne and Nora don't do that. They believe we're big enough to be told the truth.'

'That's nice of them,' said Abby. 'I bet they're worried too.'

'Probably,' Chris replied. He considered this for the first time as they sat and thought about all that had happened to them over the last few days.

'Time to get up, you two,' said Mum from the doorway, smiling at her two kids dozing on the same bed.

'Okay, Mum,' Chris replied.

'Woof,' barked Dog, but Mum didn't seem to notice.

'Come on, let's get some breakfast,' Chris said but for once Abby wasn't enthusiastic about food.

They followed Mum downstairs to the kitchen. Abby sat quietly at the table as Chris helped Mum make breakfast. 'Is there a plan for today?' she asked.

'I think we're going to play in the garden,' Abby said.

'That'll be nice. Did you enjoy your walk yesterday?'

'Yes, there was loads to see,' said Chris.

Abby giggled.

'What's so funny, you little monster?' asked Mum, ruffling Abby's hair.

'She spent more time doing handstands than looking at things.' Chris gave Abby a look behind Mum's back. He didn't want his sister to start talking about magic and crossing worlds.

'I like doing handstands.'

'Indeed you do.' Mum smiled. 'Come on, eat up.'

There was a knock on the door and Mum looked startled. 'I swear they're getting earlier.' She went to answer the front door at the same time as Tabitha wandered through the wood of the closed back door. The ghost cat sauntered over to Abby and leapt into her lap.

'Tabitha,' screeched Abby, jumping with shock at the cold sensation of the ghost cat touching her. Her cereal spilled across the table.

'What is going on?' Mum asked from the doorway. Nora stood behind her, frowning as Tabitha leapt away from the falling cereal.

'Sorry, Mum.' Chris interrupted his sister before she spoke about her ghost cat. 'I'll clean it up.'

Daphne helped Chris tidy up as Mum finished her breakfast. Chris wasn't sure, but he could have sworn that Nora aimed a kick at Tabitha as she sat down next to Abby. Tabitha gave Nora a regal stare and stalked out through the middle of the closed kitchen door.

'I'll put the kettle on,' Daphne offered.

'Thank you, Daphne. I think I've got time for a cup of tea,' Mum said.

'I'm sure you'll have time,' said Daphne, giving Chris a wink.

* * *

It was another beautiful day. The sun was shining and Abby was turning cartwheels and climbing her tree. Chris practised his football, happy to be doing something normal even if a ghost dog was happily watching him

Chapter 13

from next to the goalposts.

'Can I play?' asked Abby.

'Sure,' said Chris. They played together, taking turns in goal with only the normal level of argument about what was fair. Chris was on his toes as Abby approached with the ball at her feet; although she didn't practise as much as her brother she was pretty good. The ball flew from her foot and slotted into the bottom corner of the goal just past Chris's outstretched fingers.

'Goal,' she cheered happily. 'Can we play catch now?'

'Okay,' said Chris, shaking his fingers that stung from where the ball had skimmed across them.

'I'll get the frisbee.' Abby ran off to their playhouse.

Chris waited patiently. He was surprised at how long it took her. He took a step towards the shed – and then he heard the shout.

'Bad kitty!' shouted Abby with a distressed wail.

Chris was shocked by what he saw when he arrived at the shed door. Abby was clutching her head with one hand, but her attention was focused on a pale, sabre-toothed tiger that was cowering in the corner.

'Are you alright?' whispered Chris, not wanting to attract the attention of the powerful-looking ghost.

'Yes.' Abby didn't turn away from the creature. 'How dare you?' she demanded, approaching the tiger which was protecting one of its front paws. It gave Abby and Chris an appraising look before its eyes flashed and it faded away.

'Daphne! Nora!' Chris shouted.

'What's going on here?' Nora suddenly appeared behind the children.

'Abby just saw off a sabre-toothed tiger,' said Chris admiringly. 'But I think she's hurt.'

'Let's have a look, dear.' Daphne moved Chris out of the way and walked across to Abby.

'I...' Abby didn't seem to know what to say.

'Come on.' Daphne gently pulled away Abby's hand and looked carefully at her head.

Chris was about to rush to his sister's side but Nora was holding him back. 'Give her a second,' she whispered into his ear. 'Let Daphne show her first.'

'Show her what?' Chris asked nervously.

Daphne reached into her carpet bag and produced a hand mirror and gave it to Abby so she could look at her own face. 'I don't understand,' Abby said.

'It's a ghost wound,' Daphne explained. 'It's rare for a ghost to be foolish enough to attack living people. The energy of a living body burns too hot for the ghost's body to cope with, but they can wound us or at least leave a scar like this.'

'Abby!' Chris wriggled free of Nora's grasp and rushed to his sister. He stopped in front of her and she looked up, holding her hair away from her face to show her brother the scars the sabre-toothed tiger's claw had left on her forehead.

'Pretty cool, isn't it?' she said with a broad smile.

'Erm,' Chris didn't know what to say. It was all too much of a shock.

'It's mostly in the hair line,' said Daphne. 'And a fringe will cover the rest.'

'Does it hurt?' asked Chris, still looking at the scars.

'Not any more,' said Abby. 'It was so cold when he

Chapter 13

attacked me and I was really scared but then I realised he couldn't really hurt me, so I got cross.'

'So what are ghost wounds?' Chris asked.

Nora said, 'When a ghost attacks, they leave the ghost of a wound rather than a fresh injury, hence the scar. No one knows why. There has only been a handful of such wounds recorded in the history of magic so we don't know much about them. Don't worry, she'll be fine. It's only skin deep.'

'But what are we going to tell people?' asked Chris.

'Abby was attacked by a cat as a child. The scars have grown as she has,' said Daphne. There was a strange tone to her voice and as she spoke Chris could feel the words take on a life of their own.

'I've always had it,' said Abby, with a mischievous grin. Chris had an image of Abby's party trick with new people. 'Look at my scar,' she would say, holding back her hair to startle them, laughing when they didn't know what to say.

'Is that really going to work?' asked Chris.

'Some lies carry their own truth,' Daphne said. 'And stories have their own power, they barely need any magic to change history.'

Chris looked at Nora but she shook her head, 'Don't look at me, lad. This is Daphne's area of expertise, not mine.

'Let's have some tea,' said Daphne, so they did.

* * *

Chris was waiting anxiously in the kitchen when Mum came home. Abby skipped in with her hair scraped back in a ponytail, showing off her new/old scars.

'Can't you cover them up?' said Mum.

'But they're cool,' replied Abby.

'I'm only worried about shocking other people,' said Mum. 'I wish I had your bravery.' She gave Abby a fierce hug and kissed her scars.

Chris looked at Daphne, who gave him an amused wink; with that, Chris understood that Abby's scars had been magically woven into their family history.

CHAPTER 14

An Escalating Situation

'A sabre-tooth tiger,' said Daphne later that evening, still in awe. 'Where on earth did that come from?'

Nora looked at her across their kitchen table and shook her head. She shared her friend's concern but she also had her suspicions about the afternoon's visitor. 'I think someone else is involved,' she replied. 'I don't think you progress from family pets to pre-historic predators as part of a natural sequence. My guess is that the first ghosts are the disturbed spirits of pets buried in the garden, probably beneath the children's shed. The children are accessing some source of magic to give form to those spirits, but we can't locate it. Now all of a sudden there's a ghost sabre-tooth tiger; not only that, it was prepared to attack the living. That has to be a new development.'

'Was Chris too far away? The boy has a natural talent.'

'But no training,' replied Nora. 'Much as he wants it.'

'He does?'

'Yes, he does. I might need your help with that.'

'I'm not sure I can help with someone with as much talent as he has. Even untrained, he'll instinctively resist any attempt to alter his will,' said Daphne. 'Even if it is for his own good, anything I would be prepared to do would not last.'

'We'll have to go over there tomorrow. If random spirits are being drawn to the garden, who knows what could turn up next.'

'You're up to something.' Daphne eyed her friend suspiciously. 'We could take the children away and that should solve the problem but you have a theory, don't you?'

'I wouldn't go that far,' said Nora carefully. 'But I have an idea.'

* * *

The next day started normally enough with Mum going to work and the old women watching the children but by mid-morning things were getting out of hand. There were a number of new spirits running around, much to the amusement of the children.

Nora was getting worried. 'We're going to have a real problem on our hands soon.'

'More than this?' Daphne asked, pointing at the handful of ghost animals.

'There's no telling what could be attracted here,' Nora replied. 'Or awoken,' she muttered under her breath.

'Can I take the children away now?' Daphne demanded.

'Take us where?' Abby asked. Chris was close behind her.

'Away from this madness, my dear,' she said, turning to face Abby, 'I don't like having the two of you around these spirits when we don't know what is going on.'

Chapter 14

'They seem harmless today,' said Chris, looking thoughtfully at a wolf skulking in the bushes.

'So far,' said Daphne. She looked at Abby. 'But we've already had one incident too many.'

'Chris...' said Abby.

Chris saw that his sister was putting on a brave face and didn't know what to say.

'We think it's for the best,' Daphne said.

'You do,' replied Chris, watching Nora. 'But what about Nora?'

'Clever,' replied Nora. '*We* do. I need to see what happens when you two are taken away but I'll need you soon, so don't run off.' Nora nodded curtly to Daphne and wandered down the garden.

'Come on, dears,' Daphne said cheerfully. 'I've got something to show you, Chris. It should cheer you up.'

'What about me?' asked Abby.

'I'm sure we'll think of something.'

* * *

Chris stood in the room and was amazed. The walls were lined with bookshelves that contained books and leather folders filled with papers. There were several animal skulls in a cabinet and a plastic human skeleton in the corner wearing a trilby hat at a jaunty angle. There was an old-fashioned globe by a solid oak desk upon which a sleek computer rested.

'The hat was Daphne's idea.' Nora shook her head ruefully and sat behind her desk.

'I like it,' replied Chris.

Nora continued. 'So, the good news is that the rate of

new arrivals has slowed since Daphne left with the pair of you.'

'And the bad news?'

'Your garden is still over-run by ghosts and it's getting worse. We'll have to do something about it.'

'What do you mean? I thought you didn't know what was happening.'

'We still don't but there's too much magic being attracted to one place. I still can't find the source of it. There are too many ghosts surrounding your shed and I am worried what else might come to investigate. We can't stop the spirits but we can contain them.'

'How?'

'By creating a protective circle around the shed. I'll need your help.'

'Me?' said Chris incredulously. 'What can I do?'

'The new ghosts are weaker. Their spirits are older and I don't think they are gaining their power from Abby or you but they have been attracted by your ghosts, like moths to a flame. I think we can use the link you have with that ghost dog of yours to place a protective spell.'

'I don't understand.'

'This isn't as simple as creating a circle around an object. It is question of *when* as well as *where*. By using your memory of calling Dog out of the spirit world, and using your magical signature, I can create a better protective spell around the shed. The circle won't be impenetrable, but it will hold for a while and I'll learn a lot about anything that tries to cross it.'

Chris felt a little lost and yet there was a certain logic to what Nora was saying. 'I have a magical signature?'

Chapter 14

Nora nodded, picking up a stone from her desk. 'Magic flows through its user. Every action has its equal and opposite reaction. When we use magic, even unintentionally, magic uses us. There is both give and take. Because we are all different, we all use magic – and are used by magic – differently.'

'So what do we do?'

'More research but we need to gain some time so we can contain the situation. Will you help me?'

Chris didn't feel like he had any other option. 'What about Abby?'

'She'll stay here with Daphne. I need you to promise me one thing.'

'What's that?' asked Chris.

'That you'll do exactly what you are told.'

* * *

Chris was surprised when Nora handed him what she called a meditation stool, a short wooden bench with two legs. She showed him how to kneel on the floor and place the stool behind him so he could sit back and put his weight on the stool rather than on his ankles. His hands rested on his knees as he kept his back straight and his gaze level.

'Every object and action is important in ritual magic so pay attention to your breathing and listen closely to what I say.'

Chris felt strangely calm but extremely self-conscious. Nora's stream of instructions was not how he had expected magic to be performed.

'Close your eyes and focus on the movements of your

belly as you breathe in.'

Chris heard Nora strike a match and smelt a spicy perfume as he drew in air through his nose. His shoulders relaxed as he breathed out through his mouth. After a few breaths he felt peaceful, although his brain was buzzing and his skin tingled.

'Picture your house. See it in front of you. Solid. Home. Where is Dog?'

'He is sitting at the end of our path waiting for me,' Chris whispered.

'Good,' said Nora. 'And where am I?'

'Kneeling in front of me,' replied Chris. As he said this, he could see Nora striking a bell that rang deep and warm but he didn't lose sight of his house.

'Reach out to Dog. Tell him to go to the back door. Under no circumstances is he to move from the back step.'

For a moment Chris tried to talk silently to his pet but an instinct took over and he imagined Dog hearing what to do.

'Keep your attention on Dog and me,' said Nora. 'Do you trust me?'

'No,' said Chris, telling the truth without hesitation.

'Good boy,' said Nora.

Chris felt a strange cold sensation behind his eyes and in his brain. 'Ow.'

'Breathe, boy,' Nora said, sounding both calm and concerned.

Chris tried to focus but his concentration was fading and then he was a passenger in his own body. A sharp pain, driven deep into his brain, held his attention and his

Chapter 14

whole body slipped away from him as the world fell into a dream. He could feel his lips moving but he had no control over the words that left them as he floated, trapped, while Nora continued the spell. He stayed like this until Nora was finished and he could be allowed to go to sleep.

CHAPTER 15

Back to Normal

Chris awoke to find himself lying on a battered old sofa, wrapped in a blanket. Abby was watching him anxiously. 'He's awake,' she called.

'There you are, dear.' Daphne poked her head round the living-room door. 'Would you like some milk and sandwiches?'

Chris's body ached but he also felt hungry and nodded weakly.

'Are you okay?' asked Abby when they were alone. 'They wouldn't tell me what happened.'

'I think so.' Chris sounded very weak.

'Chris?'

'It's okay Abby,' he said. 'It was hard work.'

'What was?'

'Magic,' he said grimly, closing his eyes and drifting back to sleep.

'He's gone back to sleep,' Abby whispered, as Daphne came in with a tray laden with sandwiches wrapped in foil and a jug of iced goat milk.

'He'll be back to normal soon enough.'

'The lad will be fine,' Nora said, following her friend

Chapter 15

into the room.

'What did you do to him?'

'He's just tired. It was a hard spell,' Nora said.

'Like I told you, dear, we had to do something.'

'The ghosts weren't doing anything wrong,' said Abby. 'It's not their fault.'

Nora and Daphne shared a look but didn't say anything. Chris stirred and his eyes slowly opened.

'I brought you some food.' Daphne put her tray down on a table by the sofa.

'I'm so hungry,' Chris said weakly, forcing himself to sit up. He gave Nora a hard stare. 'Did it work?'

'Yes,' she replied.

'Good. Can you pour me some milk, please, Daphne?'

'Of course, dear. You have to rest up.'

Despite his tiredness, Chris demolished his first sandwich and gulped down half a glass of milk.

'Take your time,' said Nora curtly. 'No one is going to take it from you.'

'Sorry.' Chris looked up with a rueful smile. He ate the next sandwich slowly and took a sip of milk before asking, 'So what happens now?'

'We wait,' said Nora quietly.

After Chris had eaten they went back to their own house, which now seemed strangely calm. Dog was waiting patiently for Chris on the back step but it was Daphne who opened the door and called him in. For a moment Abby was scared for Tabitha and Fluffy, but then her ghost cat came sauntering down the garden, walking around their shed with Fluffy leaping ahead of her.

'Can we use the shed?' asked Chris. He looked closely

but couldn't see anything different about it, although Tabitha was walking in a wide semi-circle around it.

'Not at the moment,' said Nora.

Chris remembered that Nora had needed the shed to place the protective spell in the garden, like the spell was tied to it and lay around it in a circle. He wondered how she had the strength to do what she had done.

'Let's get you set up in the front room,' said Daphne, leading Chris away.

'I'm going to play.' Abby skipped outside and ran to her tree.

Nora watched her run round the shed with satisfaction, then followed Chris and Daphne.

'What did you do?' Chris asked her.

'I had to borrow your body,' said Nora. 'I'm sorry. You would have stopped the spell from working so I had no choice. Performing that spell with someone untrained was dangerous for both of us.'

Chris nodded. 'I think I understand.'

'You stay here and watch a film.' Daphne wrapped Chris in a blanket. 'We'll tell your mother that you were sick this afternoon.'

'You should rest up tomorrow as well,' said Nora. 'The spell will have taken a lot out of you. The pair of you will be safe for now, but we'll keep watch.'

* * *

Mum came home to find Chris dozing on the sofa and Abby outside playing in the garden as usual.

'He started to feel ill this afternoon,' Daphne said. 'Nothing serious.'

Chapter 15

'Poor love,' said Mum. 'I was planning to take tomorrow off anyway.'

'That sounds nice,' replied Daphne.

'You've been a real help,' Mum said. 'But you should have a rest and it will be nice to have a long weekend.'

'They've been no trouble, dear,' said Daphne. 'None at all.'

'Well, you must be doing something right. We left a string of exhausted babysitters back in London.'

'There's no substitute for experience,' Daphne smiled.

'Do you have children?'

'No,' said Daphne. 'But I was part of a big family so there were always plenty of other people's children to look after.'

'That must have been nice.'

'It was.' Daphne sounded wistful.

* * *

Chris went without eating, although they didn't tell Mum that this was because he was still full of Daphne's food and drink. Mum treated Abby to fish fingers and chips with mushy peas. Abby was sitting at the table when Fluffy came flying in through the back door and shot through the room. Next, Tabitha came slinking in and settled nervously behind the little girl.

Mum bent down to take dinner out of the oven. As she did so, a huge dinosaur head came through the wall and snapped at where Mum's head would have been if she was standing up.

Abby clapped a hand over her mouth to prevent a scream as the ghost creature roared in frustration. Its teeth were huge but it could only get its head into the room. Through the kitchen window Abby saw the dinosaur's huge body with its tail stretching back through their playhouse and down the garden. The ghost's arms waggled comically as it roared again but, unlike the friendly ghosts, it barely made a sound. The worst that happened was that its breath ruffled Mum's hair. The ghost recoiled in horror as Abby's mum stood up with a tray of steaming hot chips; it looked at Abby for a second and then faded.

'Are you okay? You look like you've seen a ghost,' Mum said. She couldn't understand why Abby started to giggle.

* * *

Nora cried out in pain and held onto a chair for support.

'What is it?' asked Daphne.

'A T-Rex, an actual dinosaur.' Nora couldn't hide the wonder in her voice.

'How on earth did it get round the spell?'

'It didn't. Somebody forced the poor ghost to try but it couldn't cross. A dinosaur was big enough to reach the house but couldn't do any damage. Whoever was controlling it wasn't strong enough to break the spell and couldn't keep trying for very long.'

'So we're no better off?' asked Daphne.

'I wouldn't say that. Whoever it was won't be trying again any time soon. They also have to be very skilled with magic.'

'I know that look of yours. I wouldn't want to be whoever it is who crossed you.'

Chapter 15

'That poor spirit deserved better. It's never good to use power like that over anything.'

'Will the boy feel anything?' Daphne looked concerned.

'I protected him as much as I could,' Nora said. 'But there was only so much I could do.' She sat down heavily, although she didn't relax; many years of practice made sure she remained in control.

'I fancy some tea.' Daphne made herself busy to prevent herself from fussing over her friend.

'I'll have a cup if you've got the kettle on.'

* * *

Abby counted to a hundred after Mum had tucked her in then sneaked into Chris's room, climbing onto his bed and ruffling Dog's ear. Chris was curled into a ball and wrapped tightly in his sheet; both of his arms were tucked into his chest as if he was in pain. 'You awake, Chris?'

Chris opened a tired eye. 'I am.'

'I saw a dinosaur,' Abby said excitedly.

'A dinosaur?' Chris sat up slowly. 'What do you mean a dinosaur?'

'Mum was getting dinner out of the oven and it tried to eat her.'

'You're not making any sense, Abby,' said Chris crossly, rubbing at his eyes. 'Was it a ghost?'

'Of course, silly.' Abby giggled.

'But what about the spell?'

'The ghost faded really quickly,' Abby replied sadly. 'It looked so cross, even for a dinosaur, and then it disappeared. I haven't seen any others.'

Chris tried to make sense of what his sister was telling him but he was exhausted. His body ached and a horrible pain in his chest seemed to stretch up into his brain. He rubbed his eyes again, hoping the world would come into focus. 'I'm sorry, Abby. I don't feel very well.'

'It's okay, I'll look after you.'

CHAPTER 16

Taken

Mum brought Chris breakfast in bed. The dry toast helped to settle his stomach but he still spent most of the morning dozing. Abby and Mum were in the garden, Abby investigating and exploring while Mum worked out what she would do with all the new space they now had.

'What are you doing?' Abby skipped up to Mum as she investigated an overgrown border.

'Seeing if we have anything in these beds that can be rescued but I have no idea what is a weed and what is a plant.' Mum straightened up and stretched.

'Daphne could tell you, she knows all the plants,' said Abby confidently.

'I'll have to ask her,' said Mum, stifling a yawn.

'Do you want to play catch?'

'In a bit,' said Mum. 'I'm so tired, I'll have to sit down for a while but I will later.'

'Promise?'

'Yes, you monster.' Mum gave Abby a tired hug.

'Okay.' Abby skipped away and turned a cartwheel before running back down the garden.

Mum shook her head, amazed by her daughter's

energy. She sat down against Abby's tree, leaning against the warm trunk and enjoying the sun on her face. She slowly drifted off to sleep, listening to her daughter talk to her imaginary cat.

* * *

Abby was quite to content to play for about ten minutes, then she ran back towards the border where she'd left her mum. 'Mum,' she called. 'Mum!' But no matter how loudly she shouted, her mum did not reply. Abby was scared. She ran back to her tree but Mum wasn't there. Abby's heart thudded in her chest; she had seen her mum sleeping under the tree only a moment ago. She didn't know what to do so she ran to her brother's room, shouting his name.

'What is it?' asked Chris, as his sister burst into his room.

'Mum's gone. She was under my tree and now she's not there any more.'

'Abby, calm down. I don't understand. Maybe she's gone to do something or gone to the loo.'

'No,' Abby wailed. 'Something bad has happened.'

Chris raised his voice to get his sister's attention. 'Look, we're going to do a proper search and if we can't find her we'll get Nora and Daphne.' Abby nodded, calming down slightly. 'Now give me a minute to get dressed and then we'll get started. Dog.'

'Woof,' barked Dog, who was sitting at the end of the bed, looking alert.

'Find Mum,' Chris ordered. Dog leapt off the bed and scampered away through a wall.

Chapter 16

Chris got dressed, then he and Abby searched the house and garden, calling for Mum. She was nowhere to be found – and Dog seemed to have disappeared too. Chris did not like that at all.

'Where is she?' asked Abby quietly.

'I don't know,' Chris admitted. 'But we need help. Come on, let's get Daphne and Nora. They'll know what to do.'

Chris and Abby ran down the road and up the little path to the old women's house. Before they could knock on the door, it opened to reveal a curious Daphne. 'Hello, what are you doing here?'

'Mum's disappeared,' Abby cried. 'We need your help.' She pushed past Daphne and headed to the kitchen.

Daphne looked at Chris. 'We'd better talk about this,' she said, waving him in. They followed Abby into the kitchen. As they sat down round the table, Nora came in from the garden.

'So what happened?' she asked Abby.

'I was playing in the garden and Mum was asleep under my tree and then she wasn't there any more.'

'We've done a proper search but we can't find her,' Chris said earnestly.

'I see.' Nora shared a look with Daphne. 'I was worried about something like this.'

'You what?' asked Chris incredulously.

'I felt what happened with that dinosaur last night,' replied Nora.

'Well I didn't,' said Daphne. 'But I recognise an abduction by the Fairy King when I hear about one.'

'The Fairy King?' Chris looked as confused as his

sister.

'The legend is so old you wouldn't know it, dear,' Daphne said. 'When we were children, no one would dream of sleeping under a sacred tree. You would be insulting the King of the Fairies and he would have the right to take you to his court for punishment. Now is not the time to be teaching you ancient tree lore, but you'll have to go after them. The only way to get your mother back is to go to the Land of Fairy.'

'Mum was abducted by fairies?' I thought they were nice.'

'I am sorry Abby,' said Daphne, 'but that is not really true. It depends what stories you read, but fairies have very powerful magic which has always made it dangerous for others to deal with them.'

'Your oak tree is a sacred tree,' Nora said, continuing the explanation. 'It all makes sense now. There should be no links between the Land of Fairy and this world, but somehow the Fairy King has managed to hide this one sacred tree for thousands of years. That is the source of magic that we couldn't find: a link back to the Land of Fairy right next to a pet graveyard. That is why you were able to create familiars like Dog and Tabitha. It will have been the king who forced the sabre-tooth tiger to attack you, Abby.'

'And who tested the protection spell with the ghost of the largest animal he could find.' Chris now understood what had happened to him last night and why he felt so bad this morning; he could feel the spell whispering the truth to him.

'Indeed.' Nora nodded, looking at Chris thoughtfully.

Chapter 16

'But why do we have to go? You are the ones with the magic.'

'We can't go there,' Daphne said sadly.

'Separation from the magical lands was part of the peace agreement,' said Nora. 'We can't travel to another world with magic without being invited.'

'But the king broke the terms'

'That does not allow us to simply ignore them.' Nora said, watching Daphne lay a consoling hand on Abby.

'But what can we do?' Abby demanded.

'You can go there, for a start,' said Daphne.

'But…'

'No buts, Chris.' Nora's voice was stern. 'I'm not going to lie to you. The Land of Fairy is a dangerous place but you must go there if you want to get your mother back. We'll prepare things here as best we can for you, but the pair of you must go. And the sooner you get there, the better.'

Abby was wide-eyed with fear but she gave a determined nod.

'So what do we do?' Chris asked, his voice surprisingly firm.

'We will trick the Fairy King into abducting you but we can interfere with the process. You will be in the Land of Fairy but, crucially, you will arrive *outside* his court and so will have a chance to find help and attempt a rescue.'

Chris and Abby looked uneasily at Nora as she continued.

'You have to go to the Land of Fairy, but this way it will be on your terms. You can then gather any allies you can find and challenge the king to a contest.'

'No fairy can resist a game,' Daphne explained.

'Fairies are tricky creatures but they can't resist a game or challenge,' Nora said. 'More importantly, you will have the right to set the rules. They will try to bend these rules as much as possible but if you set the rules carefully enough they won't be able to get round them.'

'Ask for the return of your mother and a safe passage home,' said Daphne. 'If you just ask him to free your mother, you will all be stuck in the Land of Fairy and the king will find some other way to make you his.'

'Okay,' said Chris. 'Is the king the only way we can get back?'

'I don't know,' said Nora, 'When I was learning the craft, you only had to persuade a single fairy to help you, but towards the end they started working together towards a common purpose.'

'It was so strange,' said Daphne. 'Fairies loved tricking each other as much as anyone else, especially in the Land of Fairy, so why they started working together is a mystery.'

'Why was it better in Fairy?' asked Abby. The old women looked at Abby, and she seemed to shrink a little but continued. 'I just meant, why was it better to trick people in the Land of Fairy?'

'The Land of Fairy is a very magical place,' said Daphne, closing her eyes as she spoke the ancient lore. 'When you enter that land, your true nature is heightened. With careful control, you can keep this true self hidden but it is there for anyone to find. It is your last hope and best escape, but tread warily. And be prepared, for the locals are restless.'

Chapter 16

'What's that supposed to mean?' asked Chris.

'That they should be just as scared of you as you are of them, but they won't be,' said Nora, with relish, 'If you hide your true natures from the fairies they won't see your power and will underestimate you.'

'How are we going to learn what we need to?' asked Chris. 'We don't have powers.'

'The Land of Fairy heightens your existing skills. Your true natures will show themselves thanks to the quantity of magic floating around. Use what you already know and you will be better at it,' replied Daphne.

'Your familiars will help,' said Nora. 'Dog is already in the Land of Fairy. I felt him cross when you sent him to look for your mum. Tabitha will go with you but she will look after herself above anything else. Typical cat...'

'They can't help their nature,' said Daphne. 'Particularly in the Land of Fairy.'

'Time to get going,' said Nora. 'Time flows differently between worlds. There's no knowing how long your mother has been in the Land of Fairy. We don't want to get her back and find she's my age.'

'I don't think that's possible,' said Chris, staring at Nora with understanding and wondering just how many years she had lived.

'Indeed,' she said, nodding at him approvingly.

CHAPTER 17

A Strange Land

The four of them walked to Abby and Chris's house where they found Tabitha in the front garden waiting for their return.

'Now, you're to go with them and give them all the help they need,' Daphne said to Tabitha, looking at the pale cat with a smile.

'I'll know if you don't,' Nora said sternly.

Tabitha looked from Daphne to Nora, then stood up and rubbed herself against Abby's leg. Abby scratched her ears.

'Hmm. Come on then,' said Nora.

They walked round the house but paused when they reached the back garden.

'We shouldn't say anything important by the tree,' Daphne said. 'Do you have any last questions?'

'Should we take anything with us?' asked Chris.

'Nothing would cross over with you,' replied Daphne.

'There's so much magic in the Land of Fairy that you'll find what you need,' said Nora. 'But be careful; a fairy's main interest is itself.'

'I'm scared.' Abby squeezed Chris's hand.

Chapter 17

'Good,' said Nora. 'That will keep your minds sharp.'

Abby looked at Daphne for reassurance. 'Trust your instincts and work as a team. You'll be fine, dear,' Daphne said.

'Now this is what we are going to do,' said Nora.

* * *

They approached Abby's tree in silence. It seemed to loom over them with evil intent.

'Go on, lad,' Nora said inside Chris's head. He led his sister to the tree trunk and they turned. The old ladies were walking towards the back door, although Chris knew that they were watching carefully.

Chris and Abby sat on the grass and leant against the rough bark of the tree trunk. Tabitha settled down between them, pressing her ice-cold fur into their legs. Chris closed his eyes and tried to clear his mind as Nora had taught him. Abby squeezed his hand twice and then he felt her relax.

It felt as if the world stopped on its axis for a moment then everything began to spin. There was the horrible smell of rotting wood surrounding them and a mighty pressure enveloped them. Chris panicked; he tried to breathe deeply but his body wouldn't respond. There was a sudden jarring as he felt Abby and himself being pulled in opposite directions. He tightened his grip on his sister's hand but felt her slipping away.

'You hold on to your sister, Christopher Aragorn Cromwell.' At Nora's command his hand responded automatically. He felt the frustration of another creature's will being thwarted by the cold steel of Nora's focus. In the background, he heard Daphne whispering words he did not understand and then the pull on Abby was released.

Suddenly Chris and Abby were flung into a tree and tumbled to the floor in a heap. A large bush broke their fall. They were on their own.

'Are you okay?' asked Abby.

'I think so.' Chris opened his eyes and looked around. He gasped as he saw the trees looming over head and felt a millipede scuttle across his hand. They were in a jungle. A huge red dragonfly, as big as his head, flew past with its wings buzzing loudly.

'How very interesting,' said an elegant female voice.

Chris and Abby turned to see a wild cat approaching them, her stripes merging with the dappled light of the jungle.

'Tabitha?' asked Abby.

'Indeed,' said the cat, as she stalked towards them.

'You're alive!'

'Many things are possible here,' replied Tabitha, stopping in front of them. 'But I don't know what those two old ladies were thinking of when they sent you.'

'You're meant to help us,' said Chris, sitting up.

'Now, you're to go with them and give them all the help they need,' said Tabitha, in a flawless impersonation of Daphne. 'I'll know if you don't,' she finished, sounding exactly like Nora and giving the children the old woman's stern stare.

'But...' said Abby, while Chris watched the cat suspiciously.

'They were right. What few talents you have will be

Chapter 17

strengthened by being here but you are so innocent that you will not be able to hide anything from the king in his own land. I have no intention of being caught helping the pair of you when I have a second chance at life with a new body in perfect health but I will do what I can. Stand up.'

Chris and Abby stood up. Tabitha walked round them and this time her fur was warm against the skin of Abby's calf as she brushed past.

'Your best defence is to remember what you are – a pair of children in a strange land with no prospect of rescue and no escape.' Abby seemed to get smaller as Tabitha spoke. 'The witches haven't spoken to you of your souls so I will not either. It will only lead to…'

Tabitha stopped suddenly. She stood perfectly still for a moment, staring into the distance and listening intently.

'Only lead to what?' asked Chris.

'Too late,' said Tabitha, leaping into the air and bounding away.

'Tabitha,' called Abby.

'Good luck,' was the cat's only reply.

Chris and Abby looked at each other in shock. 'What's going on?' Abby asked.

'I don't know,' replied Chris. 'But I have a feeling we've just found out why Nora is not keen on cats.'

'So what do we do now?'

'Find the Fairy King's court.' Chris looked around. 'But I have no idea how.'

'What was that?' Abby heard a noise in the jungle.

'I think that's what Tabitha was running away from.'

'Shall we take a look?'

'I think we need to be very careful,' Chris replied. 'I

don't think everything in this jungle is friendly and that there are worse things in these trees than fairies.'

'Then let's see what we can find.' Abby had a mischievous glint in her eye. She winked at Chris and shinned up the nearest tree, disappearing into the foliage.

'Wait for me,' Chris called as loudly as he dared. He used a trailing vine to follow his sister up the tree trunk and found her sitting on a branch waiting for him.

'At this height we'll be able pass from tree to tree without being seen from the ground. If we're quiet, we should be able to sneak up on anyone on the ground.'

'Who put you in charge?' asked Chris, but he was impressed with Abby's thinking.

'No one,' replied his sister, sticking out her tongue. 'It's just obvious.'

Chris thought about what Daphne and Nora had said. 'I'm not going to argue with you about trees, not here.' He pointed for Abby to lead the way. She scampered up a little more, made her way across a branch and leapt into the next tree.

Abby waited for a second, listening intently and reminding Chris of Tabitha, before waving for Chris to follow her. He scrambled to her side. Abby held a finger to her lips as a large, coal-black panther bounded up to the tree they were hiding in. It stopped and cocked its head before standing up. As it stood, the panther transformed smoothly into a fairy, its limbs changing and wings appearing from out of its back.

'Who trespasses in the Land of the Fairy King?' it asked.

Abby and Chris dare not make a sound as they peered

between the leaves. The fairy looked like a muscular human but was covered in black fur. Its head looked like a cross between a cat and a woman.

'I can smell something...' it said.

The children were too scared to move as the strange panther-fairy lolled nonchalantly against the tree. Finally, they heard a rustle in the foliage and a distant, familiar bark. Horrified, they looked down just in time to see Dog come bounding into the view, barking happily. He too had been transformed, his golden brown fur shone where the sun caught it.

'I don't think they trust me,' said the fairy, bending down and scratching Dog between the ears. 'Which shows sound judgement.'

'Woof.'

'I know, my man, but now that you're here it will be easier to sort out everything. Christopher, Abigail, would you be so kind as to come down out of that tree?'

Chris looked down again and saw Dog and the fairy staring up at them.

'What do we do?' whispered Abby

Chris looked down at his ghost dog, shut his eyes and reached out with his mind. There was nothing there but a dog's friendliness towards the strange fairy and Chris felt reassured. 'We get some help,' said Chris, beginning to climb down the tree.

CHAPTER 18

The Court of the Fairy King

Abby and Chris stood in front of the fairy, who looked a lot bigger now they were at ground level. Dog ran excitedly around their legs, barking happily.

'Allow me to introduce myself. My name is Erykah and I am at your service,' she said with an elaborate bow. 'You must be Chris and, of course, you are Abby.' She took Abby's hand and kissed it.

Erykah was tall and graceful, with powerful muscles that moved lithely under jet-black fur. A pair of amber cat's eyes looked out from an amused feline face, whiskers sweeping away from her muzzle. With every movement of her translucent wings, coal-black fairy dust fell from them.

'Hello,' said Chris, watching the stranger carefully as Abby giggled.

'I know why you are here. I am prepared to help you and will even waive my usual fee,' said Erykah.

'Why?' asked Chris.

'A good question, my young warlock,' replied Erykah, her wide smile displaying sharp feline teeth. 'The king has had it his own way for far too long. With my help, you will give him a reminder that he has not made slaves of us all.'

'How can you help us?'

'I propose two things. Firstly, I will lead you to the court of the Fairy King, Secondly, I will both hide and strengthen your true natures. If you are worthy of such gifts, they will allow you to strike at the perfect moment.'

Chris was not convinced. 'Why should we trust you?'

'Because you have no choice,' Erykah said with a broad laugh. 'You have absolutely no choice.'

Chris did not trust this strange fairy but he could think of no other way to find out where they needed to go. 'What do you think, Abby?'

'I think that if she lies to us, I will split her in two and feed her to a dragon.'

Chris was shocked at Abby's words but Erykah laughed delightedly. 'A true warrior's response if ever I heard one. We shall get on very well.' Erykah bowed once more and flapped her translucent wings, covering them in a fine layer of her coal-black fairy dust.

'Erykah!' said Chris warily, but he felt the magic flowing through him. He smiled as it whispered the secrets of fairy glamours into his mind, revealing their spells and tricks to change their appearances. Even as he pulled the magic deep into his core to hide it from the world, he could feel himself learning more and more about magic, about the Land of Fairy and fairies, about how he could use this magic to save his mother and what he was forbidden to do.

Erykah watched the children with interest as the fairy magic coursed through them. She was taken aback when

Chris spoke like an ancient magus, a magician from olden times. 'If you cross me, Erykah, you will have more to worry about than dragons.'

'But of course,' replied Erykah. 'Shall we start?'

'In a moment.' Chris laid his hand on his sister's shoulder. He could feel the magic flowing through her from the fairy dust. He gently shaped it into a small ball and hid it in Abby's warrior's heart, making sure that to any fairy observer they would appear as nothing more than scared children.

'Very good,' said Erykah, clearly impressed as all trace of their powers vanished.

Chris and Abby followed Erykah as she strolled through the jungle. Dog scouted round them at a distance. Both children were scared but they knew that they had to get their mother back.

'What are we going to do?' Abby asked.

'Leave the talking to me,' said Erykah. 'You will have enough to worry about finding the right moment to strike.'

They walked for hours though the huge trees, surrounded by teeming life. At last they saw a glow ahead and, as they approached, they heard amused laughter.

'Halt, who goes there?' The guard was a thin fairy, wearing ornate armour. He blocked their path with a highly polished spear.

'It is I, Erykah. I bring forth challengers for the king. Allow me to introduce the human children, Chris and Abby.'

'Woof,' barked Dog as he bounded back to the group.

'Challengers?' said the guard in surprise.

Chapter 18

'Indeed. Now announce us.'

The guard stared at them. Chris felt his gaze penetrating straight through Erykah but he didn't bother looking properly at the two children.

'Very well,' said the guard as he turned. 'Your Majesty and members of the court, I present the renegade Erykah who is accompanied by two human children.'

The children were shocked by the scorn with which the fairy guard announced them but Erykah didn't seem upset and motioned them onward. They stepped past the fairy guard, walked through a gap in the trees and emerged in a large clearing in the jungle.

They were standing at the edge of a perfectly circular grass meadow. Fairies were scattered like wild flowers around them; there were more near a large dais on the far side of the grass. There was a large ornate chair on the platform and behind the dais stood a familiar oak tree, but there was no sign of the king.

'Approach the throne,' said Erykah quietly. 'And ignore the bystanders.'

Chris and Abby walked slowly across the grass, Dog keeping close to Abby's heels. The distance was far greater than they expected. There was only a small gap in the canopy at the centre of the clearing. Although trees overhung the meadow, mirrors bounced what little light there was around the clearing. The light was split into coloured patterns by crystals that were suspended upon see-through ribbons tied to overhanging branches.

As instructed, the children approached the throne, ignoring the fairies who closed in around them. It was not easy as there were a lot of guards in ornate golden armour with curved swords at their waists, some of them carrying silver halberds, their axe-like blades shining on top of long ash poles. Others had curved bows over their shoulders.

A laugh rang out as the children reached the dais. 'Ah, Erykah, what have you brought me?' asked an amused but frightening voice.

'Challengers and tributes,' Erykah replied with a smile. She turned to greet all those present at court. 'Enough for me to leave this place as a free fairy.'

'We shall see about that,' the voice replied.

Chris listened carefully; he could hear something in both voices, yet he could not work out what it was. There was whispering at the edge of his hearing but he could not identify who was speaking, nor what was being said.

'We shall not,' said Erykah, suddenly stern. 'I bring you two human children, one a potential magus, and you claim this is not fair tribute?'

There was a gasp at her announcement, accompanied by a low growl from Dog. Chris was too distracted to work out why the court was so shocked. He knew that the more they kept secret, the better their chances were of finding their mother and escaping, but this treacherous fiend was already giving away some of their secrets.

'Behold, their familiar,' said Erykah, pointing to Dog, who pressed closer to Abby's ankle.

'Interesting,' said the king, appearing on his throne. The children did not see how it happened; one moment the chair was empty and the next it was not. The king's looks matched his voice. A pair of glowing red eyes stared coldly out from beneath a blue steel helmet. A blood-red cloak was draped around his armour but his face remained hidden in the shadow of his helmet. 'But what did you have in mind?'

'We've come for our mum,' said Abby.

'And safe passage home,' added Chris, remembering what they had discussed with Daphne and Nora.

'But I like your mother where she is,' the king laughed and waved behind him. Now that they were closer, the children could see a number of life-like stone statues around the old oak tree, a tree that was a perfect replica of Abby's tree in their garden back home. Under its branches, a statue of their mother slept peacefully.

'What is the life of a human worth when weighed against the untapped power of a potential magus?' Erykah asked. 'And a human one at that.'

Chris shivered but steeled his resolve. 'What are your terms, Your Majesty?'

'I propose the ancient human trial for a hero. You must pass the three tests of a true warrior. If you succeed, I will return the three of you to your world.'

'Unharmed?' asked Chris.

'You mother will be returned to you as I found her. However, if you fail even one test then I shall claim you all for my collection. You will make fine statues like your mother and shall wait here for all eternity until I can use your life force and magic to soar across the void in the age of disorder.'

'Will they be allowed to work as a team?' Erykah asked. 'They are only children, after all.'

'They can nominate the most likely to succeed, but they must face each trial alone.'

'What are these tests?' Chris was worried what the answer would be. He was sure that neither Abby nor he were true warriors yet, even though Abby had potential.

'The three tests are of courage, skill, and sacrifice. You may know no more before you undertake these trials. These are my terms, you may take them or… There is no or,' said the Fairy King, leaning forward.

'They accept,' said Erykah, looking down at Chris and Abby who were visibly shaken.

'Then let the trials begin.'

CHAPTER 19

The First Trial of a True Hero

'The first trial is a simple test of courage,' said the Fairy King, rising from his throne. 'One of you shall cross a simple bridge across this great chasm.' As he spoke, the king waved his arm and Chris and Abby found themselves on the edge of a deep valley, its edges falling away to a river of molten lava. 'You must face an enemy as you make your way across.'

Chris looked at the stone bridge that spanned the chasm; it was barely wide enough to place one foot upon and appeared to go on forever. 'How long is the bridge?' he asked.

'It depends on who steps upon it,' Erykah replied.

'I will cross it,' said Abby. There was a gasp all around them from the fairies as the small girl volunteered.

'Abby, we haven't even talked about it!' said Chris.

'Too late,' the Fairy King cried. 'The hero has been chosen.'

'That's not fair,' cried Chris, as Dog growled quietly.

'Who said these trials have to be fair?' asked the king with a laugh.

'Abby,' Chris whispered, hugging his sister as the

magic of the Land of Fairy whispered new secrets to him. 'You will have to face one of your fears on that bridge.'

'The masked man?' asked Abby, remembering with a shudder the nightmares she'd had when she had first seen a Japanese suit of armour on a trip to the local museum where they used to live.

'Maybe, but none of it is real. Fairies are masters of illusion. But I don't know how you are going to cross that bridge.' Chris was genuinely concerned about how she was going to stand on the bridge, yet alone walk across it and deal with a magical test based upon her fears.

'Don't worry, Chris, it's gymnastics,' Abby whispered in his ear. She squeezed him tightly and, once they separated, she skipped to the start of the bridge, cartwheeling to hide her fear. There was a ripple of applause in recognition of her bravery and then everyone, including Chris, held their breath.

Abby stepped onto the bridge, cautiously placing one foot in front of the other as she slowly made her way over the chasm. The wind gusted round her, trying to blow her off as she held her arms out and tried to remember all the things she had been taught at gymnastics club. She took another step and the wind died. She wobbled for a moment, trying to keep her balance, and when she looked up the world had changed around her.

The magic whispered lies to her. It told her that she was twenty-two and on a beam in the middle of an Olympic gymnastics venue. The crowd gasped and fell back into a hushed silence, everyone focused on the competitor from Great Britain. Abby's hands went over her head as she focussed on a quiet voice that whispered

Chapter 19

about all of the hours she had spent training for this one routine. The pressure of the nation was nothing compared to the expectations she placed upon herself.

Taking a breath, she performed the double cartwheel that was the next part of her routine. As she finished the second tumble, the wind gusted, the world shifted again and she was back on the stone bridge spanning the chasm. For a moment she lost her balance; she had to turn and crouch to stop herself falling and her heart pounded in her chest. It's nothing but a dance across a tree branch, she thought, skipping forward and moving faster. Her confidence returned as the hours she had spent playing in trees guided her steps.

A branch flew towards her. The wind was now howling through the largest tree Abby had ever climbed, its boughs stretching across the great chasm. Magic had changed the test again and the air was full of leaves blowing into her face as branches swiped at her. But still Abby danced her way across the branches towards the other side of the chasm. Leaping instinctively over a low sweeping branch she continued. A flash of silver made her jump back as the wind died.

'Again?' shouted Abby. Her anger turned to fear as she saw what was in front of her. A samurai sword traced a beautiful arc and an armoured warrior screamed, 'Toranaga!' and charged. The sun glinted off the fearsome face mask that had so terrified Abby when she first saw it at the museum. The bridge was wider now, which allowed the samurai enough room to stand in his armour but only just enough for him to run normally. The red-faced warrior brought down his sword in a diagonal strike and

Abby dived between his legs, kicking his exposed side as his upper body swung with his sword stroke.

With a cry of terror the warrior toppled and fell into the chasm. As Abby slipped off the bridge, it shrank back to its original size underneath her. She screamed as her hands scrabbled desperately but she managed to get hold of a ledge. She quickly tried to find another hand hold and somewhere for her feet. She slammed into the stone but somehow clung desperately to the side of the bridge.

Abby tried to catch her breath. It would be so easy to fall, she thought. Just let go and it would all be over. But although every part of her ached and she felt sick, Abby thought of her mother and from somewhere she found the strength to inch carefully back onto the narrow bridge.

It took her a moment to get her bearings but finally she was upright and ready to continue. Abby felt the stone give slightly under her foot and instinct took over. She ran as fast as she could as the bridge started to crumble behind her. The far side of the valley was in sight but she wasn't going to make it. The stone behind her was crumbling too quickly and catching up with her. With a desperate leap, she threw herself towards the far side of the valley as the bridge collapsed underneath her.

For a second Abby thought she was going to make it but the gap was too great and she fell against the chasm wall. She tumbled down the cliff face, desperately trying to find something to hold onto, before finally her leg snagged in some vines and she came to a halt.

Abby's body ached. She had torn nails and blood seeped across her face. She knew she had to get to the top of the steep cliff but first she had to stop hanging upside down. She began to swing herself back and forth until she could grab hold of another vine and pull herself across to the cliff face. Slowly Abby dragged herself up until she could free her leg and stand on a small ledge. Her knee was sore and, with tears on her face, she began to climb. She had only been on a climbing wall a couple of times, but she remembered enough to slowly make her way up.

The magic or the wind, Abby wasn't sure which, tried to whisper her doom as she climbed but Abby could tell that its power was failing. Finally her hand reached the top of the cliff and she hauled herself up, rolling away from the edge to lie exhausted on the grass.

'Abby,' cried Chris, running to his sister who was only a couple of metres in front of him. 'Are you okay?'

'Woof,' barked Dog, following behind and lapping at Abby's wounds.

Chris had watched, horrified, as his sister fought her way through the challenge. The king's magic allowed the court to follow Abby as she battled through the trial. When she reached the end, Chris found himself in the jungle clearing with no sign of the bridge or what had just happened.

'Did I make it?' Abby asked wearily.

'You were truly amazing,' said Erykah. 'But you must stand up on your own to complete the challenge. Give your sister space, Chris.'

Chris watched as his sister slowly stood up; she was in great pain but stood triumphant.

'Congratulations, you have passed the first trial,' said the Fairy King, masking his frustration with forced laughter. The members of the court applauded politely but only Chris and Erykah looked genuinely pleased. That is until Dog barked happily, wagging his tail excitedly as he bounced round in a circle, making sure no one forgot him.

The Fairy King waved a hand and Abby was surrounded by a storm of fairy dust.

'It is a healing spell,' whispered Erykah to Chris, holding him back by the shoulders, 'There is nothing to fear. She passed the trial and it is only fair that she should be healthy for the trial of skill.'

'She's not doing any more challenges,' Chris said. He was incredibly proud of his little sister but watching her go through the trial had been torture.

'Could you have done that?' asked Erykah.

'No, but it would not have been the same for me.' Chris remembered what the Fairy King had said about the differing lengths of the trial.

'Perhaps,' was all Erykah said in reply.

'So which of you dare challenge me to a test of skill?' asked the Fairy King.

'What is the trial?' asked Chris, not wanting to be tricked again.

'You get to pick the test this time and then we'll negotiate the terms,' replied the king, his cold red eyes glittering. 'Simply choose your skill or game.'

CHAPTER 20

The Second Trial of Skill

Chris stared at the tall figure of the Fairy King. He had an idea but he wasn't sure if it was a good one or not. 'I challenge you to a game of FIFA.'

'What is this FIFA?' asked the king, facing something new for the first time in centuries.

'It's a computer game,' said Chris. 'A type of game that humans play on a machine.'

'Is this a well-known game among your people?'

'Indeed it is,' interrupted Erykah, looking with amusement at Chris. 'If the game exists then it is a fair challenge and you must accept or forfeit the trial.'

'I accept,' said the king. 'But I will not agree terms until I have seen this game, if it truly exists.'

The members of the court giggled and the guards seemed to press closer.

'If you will allow me,' said Erykah. With an elaborate bow to the king, she took Chris's hands and led him round the dais to the oak tree. 'Lay your hand on the tree of power and think of what you need for this game.'

'Okay,' said Chris. The tree seemed to vibrate under his touch as he closed his eyes and thought of his game console back home.

'Very good,' said Erykah in his mind. 'But we don't have long. Is this all you need?'

'We'll need electricity to run the TV and the console,' thought Chris.

'Very well,' Erykah replied.

Chris felt the tell-tale flow of magic pass through him from Erykah and into the tree. When he opened his eyes, the TV cabinet was standing next to them, complete with the TV and games console plugged into a double electric socket that had appeared in the side of the oak tree.

'What is the nature of this game?' asked the king sceptically.

'It is based on a sport called football that humans play.' Chris turned to address the whole court as Erykah had done. 'But in this game we control all eleven members of the team. Let me show you.' He turned on the console and the TV. They worked perfectly.

'But where is the skill in this?' asked the king.

'You have to control the players that make up the team to score more goals than your opponent,' replied Chris, as the video started to play. A hush descended on the court. Chris picked up the console's two controllers and offered one to the king.

'What is that?'

'A controller,' replied Chris, careful to hide his burgeoning hope. 'It's what you use to control the game.'

The Fairy King took the controller and looked at it. He waved it experimentally in the air then muttered some words. Suddenly a stream of instructions etched in fire flowed from the controller up his arm, glowing

Chapter 20

across his armour before fading.

'I understand. I will beat you in three games or you will pass the trial,' said the king. 'All you have to do is remain undefeated.'

'That is fair,' replied Chris. 'But what team will you play?'

'I will play as the best nation from your world. You may play as whoever you like.'

'Then you'll play as Spain.'

'Let the trial begin,' said the Fairy King, turning his throne to face the TV and sitting down.

Chris faced the screen and brought up the game options. As soon as the team selection screen appeared, the Fairy King picked Spain and Chris chose Belgium. Then they moved to picking football kits. Chris was surprised when the Fairy King started to fiddle with the selection of his team but focused on setting up his side as he always did and was soon ready for the first match.

In the beginning it was a lot like playing the game with his uncle. The Fairy King passed the ball around a lot but didn't know how to break down Chris's defence and his shooting wasn't very good. Chris did a fair job of holding onto the ball when his team took control of it but mostly he quickly attacked the king's team and scored. He was 4–0 up before half time, but he saw how quickly the king was improving and he was careful not to reveal all of his tricks too soon.

At first there was a confused murmuring among the court but soon they became involved in the game and a curious quiet descended. Half way through the second half, the king intercepted an attempted pass through his defence and managed to catch Chris's team out to score his first goal. The court cheered loudly even though the king was still six goals behind; he stood to take a triumphant bow as the game showed a replay of the goal.

Chris turned to look at Abby, who winked at him. Erykah stood by her, looking on curiously.

'Woof,' barked Dog and Chris nodded in reply.

The first game finished 7–1 to Chris. His palms were sweaty and his fingers ached, which seemed odd. He wiggled his fingers as they waited for the second game to load.

'You cannot pass this trial,' said the Fairy King. 'You're as good as statues already.'

'We'll see,' Chris replied, pretending he was more confident than he felt.

The second game started and the contest was a lot more even. Chris scored first but the Fairy King soon levelled the score with a goal of his own. At the edge of his hearing, Chris could hear the first whisperings of how he would fail his mother. Just before half time, the Fairy King took his first lead with a free kick that somehow got up and over the line of players forming a wall in front of Chris's goal and then swerved round Chris's goalkeeper.

'No way,' muttered Chris quietly, as the court howled its approval of the king's lead. At half time Chris was 2–1 down and he was convinced that something was going on. Chris didn't know how the king had made the ball bend so much to score the second goal but, more importantly, the distractions that surrounded him were getting worse.

'Are you okay?' asked Abby, as Chris stood with his

Chapter 20

controller dangling from his hand while the Fairy King waited for a servant to bring him a goblet of wine.

'I think so,' said Chris, not wanting to give anything away.

The second half started and Chris's team was immediately under pressure, but he somehow managed a series of desperate tackles to stop the king scoring another goal. A garish group of dancing fairies distracted him as they flashed by and he nearly conceded a third goal, yet somehow he timed the goalkeeper's advance well enough to save the Fairy King's shot.

'Come on, Chris,' he muttered as he took a deep breath. He could feel the magic in the air as he drew it into his lungs. That's what's going on, he thought, as he focussed on the magic flowing through his body. The King was trying to distract him with magic and it was working. Chris listened to the magic of the Land of Fairy for the right spell and focussed on using the magic surrounding his hands to form a small protective spell. It was similar to the one Nora had placed around their shed and it was small enough that it passed unnoticed amongst the fairies. His hands suddenly felt much better.

Time was running out but Chris found a new confidence and a determination not to let his sister or mother down. Slowly he dragged himself back into the game and, with only a couple of minutes left, he finally broke down the king's defence and slotted home the equalising goal.

'Come on,' cheered Abby, the lone happy voice in the clearing.

Chris did not dare look round. He could feel the

magic swirling round him and he knew his focus had to remain on the game. The king tried a series of tricks with one of his players that only proved how much better he had become, but Chris managed to time a tackle perfectly and quickly counter-attacked. The perfect pass sent his winger forward and, in injury time, Chris sent a shot into the top corner.

'Yes!' he cried in relief. They kicked off and the whistle blew again straight away. Chris had won the second game.

There was only one more game to go. 'Good luck,' said Abby quietly and Chris knew he would it need it.

The game started and the Fairy King played even better. Chris could do nothing but desperately defend with as many players as possible, taking the first opportunity he could to adjust his team's tactics to protect his goal. The tension was almost unbearable and Chris knew that just one mistake would lose him the game and everything else as a result.

At half time it was still 0–0 and Chris dare not look away from the screen. The air began to swirl around him as the king laughed quietly to himself, trying some kind of magic that wouldn't quite work. Chris wondered if Erykah was helping him as much as she could.

The second half continued in much the same way and everybody watched the screen intently. A clearance broke to one of Chris's players and with a deft flick of his control stick, Chris spun his player away from a tackle and sprinted into space. This was it. Chris knew that this was his only hope and his spirits soared as his player ran towards the king's goal.

All of the king's defenders were too far away and all

Chapter 20

Chris had to do was get the ball past the goalkeeper to score. Chris watched calmly as his player reached the perfect spot and he curled the ball past the advancing goalkeeper. The score was 1–0 but Chris knew he could hold out to the end of the game. It still felt like a lifetime as the clock slowly ticked away, but finally the whistle blew and Chris had won.

CHAPTER 21

The Final Trial

'Congratulations, you have passed the second trial,' announced the Fairy King.

'Well done.' Abby rushed forward and hugged Chris.

Chris scratched Dog's ear as Erykah clapped enthusiastically but he was worried. Chris had expected the Fairy King to be furious when he lost the second trial but he seemed almost amused by the incident, as if all was going to plan.

'It is time for you to face the final trial of a true hero,' said the Fairy King grandly. 'The true test of a hero is not their courage or their skill but what they are prepared to sacrifice to achieve their goal. For the final trial, one of you must sacrifice something to me: one of you must give up your magic.'

A gasp went up from the crowd as Chris and Abby looked at each other. They could hear shocked discussions about what had been asked of them. Even Erykah lost her look of perpetual amusement.

'We must discuss this,' said Chris nervously.

'What is there to discuss?' asked the Fairy King. 'Only one of you is a potential witch. Or do you wish to join

Chapter 21

your mother in my collection of statues?'

'It is a grave decision,' said Erykah. 'They should be given time to consider what is being asked of them.'

'Very well, you shall have a few minutes. Erykah, you may draw them a circle so they have some privacy.'

Erykah nodded and started to pace round Chris and Abby, flapping her wings to release a cascade of fairy dust to form a protective dome. But Chris had seen the look on her face and knew that nothing they said in this land would remain hidden from the king.

'I will do this,' said Abby. 'I don't like magic anyway.'

'You can't.' Chris took his sister's hand and looked into her eyes. Erykah's dust floated around them and Chris had an idea.

'Everything we say is heard by the king,' Chris thought directly into his sister's brain. She nodded. 'I can't let you do this. There has to be another way.'

'But there isn't,' Abby thought in reply. 'And I'm not sad. We have to get Mummy back.'

'I could give up my magic,' thought Chris.

'No, *I* have to.'

Chris looked at his sister and saw the determination in her face. He knew there was no way to change her mind so he gave her a big hug and waited.

'I'm ready,' Abby said quietly.

'Okay,' said Chris and they turned, hand in hand, to face the Fairy King.

A glass bell tolled as the privacy spell was broken and the children found themselves in front of the dais, the court arrayed behind them and a number of guards close by.

'So what is your decision?' asked the Fairy King, his sneer half visible in the shadows of his helmet.

'I'll do it.' Abby stared up at him.

'Very good,' he replied. 'Step forward.'

Abby climbed the stairs to stand on the dais. The Fairy King stretched out an armoured gauntlet and Chris saw the magic begin to flow out of his sister. Dog growled quietly and stood next to Chris, ready to pounce. A pale glow was steadily pulled from Abby's head to the king's now-glowing hand. A few short seconds and it was done. Abby seemed to sag for a second and the king's eyes flashed.

'Seize the children,' the king commanded, making a grab for Abby.

Abby escaped the Fairy King's grasp with a move her judo teacher would have been proud of and rolled off the dais to remain out of reach. There was a gasp from the assembled court as she stood, her true nature finally revealed in the winds of the magical kingdom.

Abby had not aged but she stood more than six feet tall in her midnight-blue armour, the glow of burning stars illuminating her terrifying snarl. The ghost wound left by the sabre-tooth tiger ghost now stretched down the whole side of her face. She held a katana, a long curved Japanese sword, ready to attack anybody who came near. Her new strength meant that she barely felt the weight of the two-handed sword. Two fairy guards made the mistake of trying to follow their king's orders and found themselves disarmed in seconds.

'Hold,' said a commanding voice.

Abby's sword came to a sudden halt millimetres from

Chapter 21

the exposed throat of her foe.

'You dare confront me?' asked the Fairy King, his voice dripping with power.

'I dare,' said Chris, revealing his own true form and throwing off the guards who had tried to take hold of him. The court watched in stunned silence. The only other person making a noise was Erykah, who laughed delightedly.

The king looked upon the child who was a boy no more. Chris was dressed in dark green robes with trees etched in brown thread and in his hand he held a staff of power. He was physically unchanged but everyone could sense his magical power, just as they could see his sister's deadly skill. Chris felt the court's attention but they were mere specks to him as the magic of the Land of Fairy flowed through him unhindered, whispering knowledge and secrets as he focussed on the Fairy King.

'You would dare break your side of a fair challenge? What kind of fairy are you?' asked Chris, his voice echoing in a way no boy's ever should.

'I am the king,' shouted the Fairy King.

'But no fairy,' replied Chris, keeping his voice level. 'And so you may not sit upon the throne of this land.'

There was a general gasp from the court as Chris's words broke the many spells that the self-styled king had woven amongst the court. His appearance remained unchanged but memory began to flow back to the members of the court.

'What you say is nonsense,' replied the former king.

'No,' said Chris calmly. He could hear the babble of fairies throwing off their enchantments and, as the flow of magic increased, the land itself told him what had happened. He was unsure if it was him or the magic that spoke.

'In the beginning you gained power because it amused the court. I must congratulate you on how clever you were to make them forget who you were, but your spells are already fading. No non-fairy can hold true power over this land and you are no more part of the fabric of this realm than I am.' Chris was unsure of the magic that flowed through him, but he knew the truth of his words.

'I will not be lectured to by a mere child,' hissed the former king, pulling his sword from its jewelled scabbard. He stalked down the steps towards the children.

Chris was nervous but ready. He gripped his staff and felt the magical energy around him; spells formed in his mind. There was more than potential revealed in this place; he could feel it changing him.

The former king approached Chris first and hacked at him with a mighty swing of his sword. A simple shielding charm thickened the air in front of Chris and the blow bounced away harmlessly. The king changed tack and charged at Abby. She was ready for him; she waited until the perfect moment to strike and her blow took the former king's sword hand clean off at the wrist.

The limb fell to the floor. As it did so, a spell broke revealing a gnarled wooden hand locked round an old branch, both of which crumbled to a fine black dust in seconds. The tree spirit's true nature flickered into view for a moment before it recovered control and its previous disguise snapped back into place.

'This isn't over,' the spirit hissed, crashing across the

Chapter 21

dais. It snatched up the statue of their mother and walked into the sacred oak tree, which promptly vanished along with the spirit and their mother.

'Chris,' Abby shouted.

'It's okay,' said Chris with a calm smile. He reached into his pocket and pulled out a small plastic container. He scooped up the black powder, which was all that remained of the tree spirit's severed limb. 'We have enough here to craft what we need. That poor spirit has just made a big mistake.'

'What's that?' asked Abby, walking up to her brother.

'That tree spirit has fled to our home, a land with very little magic – except that which has been granted to the two very angry witches who are charged with keeping the peace and who just happen to be waiting for it.'

'Very good Chris,' said Erykah, clapping loudly. 'But I don't think the tree spirit is your most pressing problem.'

Dog placed himself between Erykah and the children, baring his teeth and sounding like a bear as he growled. Chris sighed deeply 'I have seen off your false king. You would think that would be enough to pay for the trip home.'

'Why would you think that?' asked Erykah with a laugh.

'You will do well as queen, Erykah,' said Chris sadly, seeing vaguely into the future. 'But there was a reason our worlds were separated.'

Chris took his sister's hand and nodded to Dog. He finally understood how Nora travelled between worlds without magic. He stepped through a dimension that many physicists on Earth would be very interested to learn about and took his sister and himself home.

CHAPTER 22

Cleaning Up at Home

Chris and Abby stepped into their back garden. The magic fell away from Abby so she shrank back to normal. The power left Chris straightaway too but the knowledge was burnt into his memory.

Daphne and Nora stood in front of them, outside a magic circle they had formed round Abby's tree. Mum was leaning back against the tree, seemingly fast asleep.

'Mum,' cried Abby.

'It's alright dear,' said Daphne. 'She's safe for now. The spirit is stuck in the tree, thanks to the circle. But we need some way to deal with him more permanently so we can rescue your mother.'

'Seems you did alright.' Nora turned to Chris as he approached.

'I think we did okay,' said Chris. 'Would some of the spirit's body be enough for you to work a spell, even if it has turned to dust?'

'That would do nicely, lad,' replied Nora.

'I don't suppose you happen to have brought some back with you, dear?' Daphne laughed.

'Might have done,' said Chris. 'Have you got a plastic

Chapter 22

bag?'

'Chris and I will sort out the spirit, Daphne.' Nora handed Chris a plastic bag. 'His relationship to his mother will help the magic.'

'Abby and I will put the kettle on,' said Daphne. 'I think everyone is going to need a cup of tea after this.'

For a second it looked like Abby was going to argue but then she turned and followed Daphne and started to tell the story of their time in the Land of Fairy.

Chris carefully scooped out the black dust from his pocket and put as much as possible into the plastic bag.

'That should do nicely. How did you get it?' asked Nora.

'Abby chopped the fairy king's hand off with a sword,' said Chris.

'Did she indeed? Very impressive.'

'But she had to give up her magic,' Chris said sadly.

'Don't tell her or Daphne, but that's probably for the best. Abby's got a warrior's soul. She'll do well enough without magic getting in her way.'

'What about me?' asked Chris. The memory of what was possible with power was still with him.

'That's going to be harder,' said Nora sadly, looking Chris in the eye.

He met her gaze and for the first time she didn't look away. Chris was fascinated as he saw a sequence of events from Nora's life pass through his mind like a film being fast forwarded. He saw her as a young girl in a tiny village, her being trained, the great magic war and the peace that followed. He felt saddened by the passing of magic from the human world and finally understood the steely determination that lay behind those old eyes.

'Uh,' he muttered, stepping back. He could feel that the same thing had happened to Nora, only she was watching a much shorter film. They looked away and, for a moment, Chris wondered what he was going to do.

'It's called a soul gaze but there aren't many with magic these days so I doubt you'll have to go through it again. Soul gazes are not to be entered into lightly. You couldn't forget what you just saw, no matter how hard you tried.' She laid a friendly hand on the boy's shoulder, knowing what a good soul the child had.

'But what do I do now?'

'We will work something out,' said Nora. 'I would have spared you this if I could.'

'I know,' replied Chris, knowing the truth of Nora's words. He'd seen into her soul and what she had lived through.

'Shall we take care of the tree spirit and get your mother back.'

'Yes. I take it there's no other way?'

'No,' replied Nora after a moment's pause. 'The spirit is too far gone. He spent too long wielding power in the Land of Fairy and won't settle in another world now. In a way, this will be kinder.'

'But he'll poison himself trapped in the tree,' said Chris.

'We don't have the strength to kill him with magic and that's not what it's for.'

'I know,' said Chris. 'I just wish there was another way.'

'So do I, but this is the other side of magic. Sometimes

Chapter 22

you have to do the things no one else wants to, not because *you* want to, but because they need to be done.'

'Let's get it over with then.'

Chris and Nora prepared what they needed for the spell in Nora's workshop and carried them to the edge of the binding circle that Daphne and Nora had placed around the old oak tree. Chris didn't need to ask why they had created the circle. From the glimpse into Nora's past, he'd seen them create it just in case it was needed.

'We were very lucky,' said Chris, breaking the silence.

'I know,' said Nora, who had seen all that had happened to the children in the Land of Fairy from her side of the soul gaze.

They nodded to each other and then they began. Nora carefully poured a circle of earth and Chris arranged a second circle of small twigs inside it. Finally, Nora created a final circle of black dust taken from the tree spirit. Chris scattered the circles with morning dew as Nora lit a candle and placed it in the centre. There should have been words but, in this moment of understanding, none were necessary as they worked together to focus their energy for the spell.

They worked the magic through Nora who, under the terms of the peace agreement, could access certain types of magic in specific circumstances. When the energy was at its height, Nora bent down, blew out the candle and lowered the binding spell Daphne and she had cast earlier. Chris slashed across the diameter of their new circle with a silver knife, focussing their spell into the blade. With a casual flick of his wrist, he sent it flying into the trunk of Abby's tree where the troublesome spirit had taken refuge. There was a dull thud, followed by a crack as the tree split where the spell took hold – and it was done.

'Thank you,' said Chris, grateful to be shown the other side of magic. Perhaps he wouldn't miss it so much after all.

'I must have nodded off,' said Mum, opening her eyes wearily. 'I've had the strangest dream.'

* * *

They were sitting round the kitchen table, sipping tea. Daphne was chatting happily, distracting Mum so she didn't notice how quiet her children were.

'I think that tree is ill,' said Daphne, pointing at Abby's tree.

Abby looked at Chris, who mouthed the word 'sorry' to her.

'We'll have to get a tree surgeon to look at it,' Mum said. 'Will you stay for dinner?'

'That'd be lovely, dear. I'll give you a hand,' said Daphne. 'Why don't you children go out to play?'

'I'll keep an eye on them.' Nora stood up slowly and followed the children outside.

Abby seemed nervous of Nora and Chris. She knew something had happened when she had left them to go inside with Daphne, but she didn't know what.

'Are you okay?' Chris asked Nora.

'I'm fine. Just old.'

'Are we safe now?' asked Abby. She looked at her tatty trainers; the Land of Fairy had not been kind to them.

'As safe as anyone can be,' said Nora. 'You certainly won't have any more magical troubles.'

Chapter 22

'Have you any magic left?' Chris was concerned for Daphne and Nora.

'Enough for our needs,' said Nora. 'And maybe for one more thing.'

What happened next would have surprised Daphne because Nora always pretended to have no gift for that particular branch of magic. With a great deal of effort, she lifted the children's spirits and pushed away their recent memories. She watched contentedly as Abby and Chris ran off to play football.

That's as it should be, thought Nora. Satisfied at last, she walked wearily to a chair and sat down for a doze, still listening to the children.

* * *

They had been playing twenty minutes when Chris heard a familiar bark in the distance. It was Dog. Chris realised that in the heat of the moment he'd forgotten about his familiar, left behind in the clearing in the Land of Fairy. The barking got closer and Chris's guilt increased until Dog burst out of a near bush and came running over to Chris. Dog had returned to being a ghost when he had left the Land of Fairy

'Woof,' he barked reproachfully.

'I'm sorry.' Chris bent down and scratched the ghost dog's cold ear. 'There was so much to do. But thank you and look – you came back.'

'Woof,' replied Dog, as if to say 'of course'.

'What are you doing?' Abby asked.

'It's Dog, he came back from the Land of Fairy.' Chris looked up in surprise and realised that Abby couldn't see the animal. 'We left him behind…'

'Aw.' Abby tried to hide how sad she was that she couldn't see Dog any more.

Chris saw that Dog was beginning to fade. He had made sure his master got home safely and now it was time to go.

'Don't leave,' Chris said quietly.

'Woof!'

'I know,' said Chris, and then Dog was gone.

Epilogue

Dad came home to find that the old oak tree that Abby loved to climb was sick and would have to go. He was surprised how well both of his children coped when the men came with chainsaws to cut it down. Chris, in particular, watched very carefully until the remains were taken away.

Abby grew up and remained true to her warrior's spirit, but that's another story. As for Chris, he went to his new school and never did learn the craft, although he remained friends with Daphne and Nora. He missed magic every day but every now and again he reminded himself there might still be time to learn.

Acknowledgements

It was not easy to get this book into your hands, and it would not have been possible without the help of the following people, all of whom made vital contributions

Firstly I have to thank Catherine Cousins and my editor Karen Holmes from 2QT Publishing. Both have dealt with more than their fair share of daft writer type questions, and this whole project would have foundered without their patience and advice. I hope that Karen found the editing process as enjoyable as I did; it certainly transformed this book for the better. My illustrator Rose Hutchings was a pleasure to work with and I owe her for bringing a part of my story to life as well as my godmother Jean for introducing us. I would also like to thank Ben Cameron and his team at Cameron Publicity and Marketing, without their help this book would likely be gathering dust in a warehouse or be lost in the digital ether.

Closer to home, my parents Pat and Chris not only fed my love of books and music as a child, but helped with project management, proof reading, and yet more capital investment into one of their children when by all rights they should be free from questions about business plans and enjoying their retirement.

Any artist needs nurturing and support. I would have likely given up years ago if it wasn't for the support, needling, and shining example set by my amazingly talented opera singing friend Sarah Cromwell. It was something she said to me whilst I was at university that led me back to writing so really any complaints should be directed towards her.

Apart from all the usual advice you can find as a writer, I found it incredibly helpful to know actual people who get paid for producing words, so I'd like to thank Sarah Ditum, Nathan Ditum and Mhairi McFarlane for setting the example of how to be both incredibly talented and thoroughly decent people. I'll have to work extra hard to make up the talent deficiency but I think I can pull off being nice, or at least fake it.

Various friends have had to listen to me talk about writing or projects without being visibly bored or rude for which I am eternally grateful, whilst one of them even produces a podcast for my sports blog, so in no particular order my thanks go to Dan, Brooke, Tony, Tewkes, Rory, Jon, Dave, Clive, Emma, Nick, Ant, and James.

None of this would be possible if my partner Rachael wasn't prepared to tolerate me tapping away at my keyboard for hours on end, plotting things in my head whilst we're out on walks, and generally being an absent minded writer. I will make it all up to you one day my love, I promise.

Finally, to any of you who have read or bought this book, thank you, I truly appreciate your time and interest. I hope you enjoyed reading it as much as I did writing it.

www.ingramcontent.com/pod-product-compliance
Lightning Source LLC
Chambersburg PA
CBHW021110080526
44587CB00010B/457